D0436731

How to Really
Love
Your
Man

How to Really

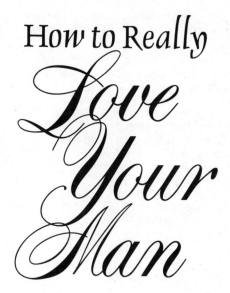

Love Your Man

Linda Dillow

THOMAS NELSON PUBLISHERS
Nashville

Published in Nashville, Tennessee, by Thomas Nelson, Inc.

Scripture quotations are from the NEW KING JAMES VERSION of the Bible. Copyright © 1979, 1980, 1982, Thomas Nelson, Inc., Publishers. Scripture quotations taken from the HOLY BIBLE: NEW INTERNATIONAL VERSION® are marked (NIV) in the text. Copyright © 1973, 1978, 1984 by International Bible Society. Used by permission of Zondervan Publishing House. All rights reserved.

Scripture quotations taken from the REVISED STANDARD VERSION of the Bible are marked (RSV) in the text. Copyright © 1946, 1952, 1971, 1973 by the Division of Christian Education of the National Council of the Churches of Christ in the U.S.A. Used by permission.

Scripture quotations taken from THE NEW AMERICAN STANDARD BIBLE are marked throughout (NASB). Copyright © 1960, 1962, 1963, 1968, 1971, 1972, 1973, 1975, 1977 by The Lockman Foundation and are used by permission.

J. B. Phillips: THE NEW TESTAMENT IN MODERN ENGLISH, Revised Edition. Copyright © J. B. Phillips 1958, 1960, 1972. Used by permission of Macmillan Publishing Co., Inc.

The Living Bible (Wheaton, Illinois: Tyndale House Publishers, 1971) and are used by permission.

Library of Congress Cataloging-in-Publication Data

Dillow, Linda.
    How to really love your man : letters to my daughters /
by Linda Dillow.
        p.   cm.
    Includes bibliographical references.
    ISBN 0-8407-3411-5
    1. Dillow, Linda—Correspondence.   2. Married women—
Correspondence.   3. Mothers—Correspondence.   4. Marriage.
5. Marriage—Religious aspects—Christianity.   I. Title.
HQ734.D623   1993
306.81—dc20   92-26407
                                                                                            CIP

Printed in the United States of America
1 2 3 4 5 6 — 98 97 96 95 94 93

$\mathscr{D}$EDICATION

To my daughters,
Joy and Robin,
and the "daughters" my sons
will bring into our lives.

CONTENTS

1

_M_Y LOVER— MY BEST FRIEND

*W*HY DO PEOPLE GET MARRIED?

Dear Daughters,

It is our anniversary, so why am I writing you instead of loving my man? The answer is simple. I'm in Vienna, and he's in Russia! Now don't feel sorry for me. We had four glorious days together last week before he left.

When you celebrate an event before the event, it still seems that you should celebrate on the "event day"! So I've decided to celebrate alone, to meditate on my marriage, to ask the hard questions, to thank God, to seek God, to evaluate if I am heading toward my goal, if I am making the right choices. How easy it is to speed through life on overdrive, never stopping long enough to reflect on who we are becoming, what our marriage is becoming.

As I reflect on my marriage, it is difficult for me to realize that my daughters are thinking about marriage. Surely, you can't be that old because that means I'm old enough to have married children! I wrote *Creative Counterpart* when I'd been married thirteen years. That many years and more have passed again so I have to ask myself, *What have I learned about loving my man? What can I share with you, my daughters, as you approach marriage that might encourage you to love your men?*

People marry for different reasons, but one man definitely takes the prize for the most unique reason! How I laughed when

I read the following advertisement, which actually appeared in the want ads of a New York newspaper: "Farmer with 160 irrigated acres wants marriage-minded woman with tractor. When replying, please show picture of tractor."

I definitely did not marry to gain a piece of farm equipment or equipment of any kind. I married your father because I wanted to be his lover and best friend forever. One of the most beautiful portions of Scripture shows us the heart of a young bride as she described her feelings for her husband. She set forth the physical attributes of her beloved and ended by saying:

> His mouth is full of sweetness,
> And he is wholly desirable.
> This is my beloved and this is my friend.
> (Song 5:16 NASB)

A perfect combination, a lover and best friend, all in one package called a husband! Recently, a woman showed me this note she had found hidden under her pillow by her husband before he left on a business trip:

Dearest Val,

Hi!!!! By now you are missing me. I want you to know that I love you and I am thinking of you even now. I miss every minute that I have to be away from you. I would much rather be holding you in my arms, pressing my lips against yours. . . .

What I miss most of all is having a good walk and talking with you. I cherish having you to talk to and share with—someone who really wants to understand me and love me. I will be back soon. I love you a LOT!!!

Your Lover,
Marc

This note graphically reveals the perfect combination: a lover whose arms and lips you long for, a best friend whose deep communication and companionship you miss.

Beginning today, your father's and my anniversary, I will write you letters and share with you all I've been learning about developing an intimate oneness with my lover and best friend. These letters will stress who we are becoming as well as what we are doing.

I will soon get to the subjects you are *most* interested in—sex, intimacy, and communication. But bear with me for a short time while I share with you some important principles concerning goals and secret choices that are necessary to create the deep relationship you long for with your man.

Where do we begin? In the beginning God created the heavens and earth. In the beginning God created man and woman. In the beginning God created marriage. *He* has the knowledge. *He* is the One who gives wisdom, who gives the power to *become*. . . .

I love you lots,
Mom

WHAT IS A PERSONAL MARRIAGE STATEMENT?

Dear Daughters,

Your father and I are considering someday retiring at beautiful Lake Tahoe. Right now it is in the dream stage but what fun to dream. As we've stayed at the Dillow family cabin at Tahoe, we've walked around and searched for lots, called realtors, even spent a morning looking at houses that were for sale! Soon we plan to have a "blueprint date" where we'll draw a plan of all the ideas that will some future day become our cabin. Knowing your father, you will not be surprised that he has ordered a computer program so we can draw the plans on the computer!

Stephen Covey, author of *The 7 Habits of Highly Effective People*, says that "all things are created twice. There's a mental or first creation, and a physical or second creation."[1] Someday, the actual physical structure of our dream cabin will be erected. But what kind of house would be built without mentally planning, measuring, developing blueprints? We have to be certain that the mental creation is really what we want. We begin with the end in view, a cabin in the woods for two with plenty of space for four children, spouses, and many grandchildren to visit.

My parents, Nana and Grandpa Dick, are mentally creating their trip to Europe for the wedding, and believe me, they have planned! A folder labeled "The Wedding" is thick with news-

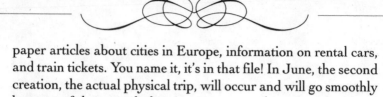

paper articles about cities in Europe, information on rental cars, and train tickets. You name it, it's in that file! In June, the second creation, the actual physical trip, will occur and will go smoothly because of the mental planning.

All of life is made up of two creations, mental and physical, the conception and the construction, even your wedding. The mental creation of this important event has gone on for months. How many brides' magazines have you read? You have done much mental creation and planning so the physical creation, the wedding, will be all you dreamed.

A good question might be: Have I put as much thought, prayer, and effort into what I want to *become* as a wife as I've put into the wedding itself? The wedding will last a few hours. Your life as a wife will last years: thirty, forty, fifty, or more.

I want to challenge you, my daughters, to spend some time in the mental creation of your personal marriage statement. I'm convinced that if each bride spent *half* the time planning her marriage purpose as she did planning her marriage party, she would become more the wife she longs to be to her man.

Too many wives live out scripts handed to them by family, friends, movies, pressures, circumstances. Either you choose a statement of purpose, what you want to become as a wife, or a pattern as a wife will be chosen for you.

As you go to bed tonight, think about the concept that all things are created twice: a mental or first creation, and a physical or second creation. Consider how you can prayerfully create *now* what you want to *become* as a wife.

I love you,
Mom

HOW TO WRITE A PERSONAL MARRIAGE STATEMENT

Dear Joy and Robin,

Many people throughout history have written personal life statements. I want to share with you two that have affected me. The first was penned by the fiery preacher Jonathan Edwards in the 1800s. I can just *feel* the strength of purpose in his words:

> Resolved, to live with all my might while I do live.
>
> Resolved, never to lose one moment of time, to improve it in the most profitable way I can.
>
> Resolved, never to do anything I should despise or think meanly of in another.
>
> Resolved, never to do anything out of revenge.
>
> Resolved, never to do anything which I should be afraid to do if it were the last hour of my life.[2]

That last resolve really goes along with living in light of time, but I would state it in a positive way: "Resolved, to strive to live each hour as if it were the last I had to live."

I sense that he adopted these resolutions after much thought and prayer. Jonathan Edwards wrote his life purpose statement

in the form of resolutions. Betty Scott Stam wrote hers in the form of prayer:

> Lord, I give up all my own plans and purposes, all my own desires and hopes, and accept Thy will for my life. I give myself, my life, my all utterly to Thee to be Thine forever. Fill me and seal me with Thy Holy Spirit. Use me as Thou wilt, send me where Thou wilt, work out Thy whole will in my life at any cost, now and forever.[3]

Betty Scott Stam lived out this prayer when she and her husband became missionaries in China and were martyred after the Communists took over in 1949. This prayer of personal life purpose has been used by many people, including Elisabeth Elliot, who copied it into her Bible and signed it when she was a young girl.

One wife chose to make her personal life statement the prayer of Saint Francis of Assisi. I have always thought it was one of the most magnificent prayers ever written and one of the most difficult to apply. I can just hear a choir singing the beautiful words as I write them:

> Lord, make me an instrument of Thy peace;
> Where there is hatred, let me sow love;
> Where there is injury, pardon;
> Where there is doubt, faith,
> Where there is despair, hope;
> Where there is darkness, light; and

Where there is sadness, joy.
O Divine Master, grant that I may not so much
Seek to be consoled, as to console;
To be understood, as to understand;
To be loved, as to love;
For it is in giving that we receive;
It is in pardoning that we are pardoned; and
It is in dying that we are born to eternal life.[4]

These prayers and resolutions are life purpose statements. I encourage you to write a marriage purpose statement so at the beginning you will know where you are heading. Think, pray, and form your thoughts into a statement, resolution, or prayer, any way you want to phrase it. It is a personal commitment between you and God, something for you to keep in the forefront of your mind, to pray about often, to use as a thermometer when you are taking your "wife temperature." This is something to review each anniversary when you thank God for your husband and for the growth in your life and relationship during the preceding year. Probably you will add things to it as the years pass.

Let me close by sharing with you my personal marriage statement, which I have compiled over many years. I will use these resolutions to form the bases of the letters I will write you about loving your man. As I said, what you write is personal, and I've never shared this statement before. But what a joy to share it with my daughters as you prepare for marriage that it might be a help and an encouragement to you.

My Personal Marriage Statement

I Choose: To seek to discover and meet the deep needs of my man.

I Choose: To seek to encourage rather than to be encouraged.

I Choose: To seek to be quick to hear, slow to speak, quick to understand, and slow to anger.

I Choose: To seek to be a creative lover.

I Choose: To seek to give rather than to receive.

I Choose: To seek to forgive rather than to be forgiven.

I Choose: To seek to live my marriage from an eternal perspective.

As I write out these choices for you, it is so evident to me that I still have a long way to go in becoming the wife God desires me to be and I long to be, but I realize, also, that because I have made these commitments before the Lord, I am much farther down the path of "becoming." Roosevelt once said, "It's not so important what a woman is as what she is becoming, for you shall be what you are now be-com-ing!" That is encouraging!

I love you,
Mom

*W*HAT IS THE DIFFERENCE BETWEEN A GOAL AND A DESIRE?

Dear Daughters,

Sarah had a goal for her marriage: to have an intimate one-ness, a close, wonderful relationship, with her husband, Sam. Being a young woman of purpose and commitment to Christ, she read every book on communication in marriage, attended seminars on being a wife, and tried harder than most to do her part to create intimacy.

After five years of marriage, Sarah was angry, frustrated, and disillusioned. Marriage was a farce. She'd tried *so hard* to communicate, but Sam, the strong silent type, grew more silent instead of sharing. The more she talked about closeness, the more he retreated. Without realizing what she was doing, Sarah gradually spent her hours and days devising plans to change "silent Sam" into "sharing Sam" so they could have the intimate one-ness that she so desperately desired and that she knew God desired. After all, He was the One who said, "The two shall become one." The more she demanded an intimate oneness, the more she and Sam grew into two separate people with a chasm between them.

My heart ached for Sarah. Her motives were right. She diligently worked on her marriage. What was the problem? What caused her anger and disillusionment? The answer is simple:

Sarah's goal, not Sarah, was wrong. Like Sarah, many of us wives have our goals and desires mixed up.

I have benefited so much from Dr. Larry Crabb's definitions of a goal and a desire because, like Sarah, I once had my goals and desires confused.

A goal may be defined as a purpose to which a person is unalterably committed. He assumes unconditional responsibility for a goal, and it can be achieved if he is willing to work at it.

A desire may be defined as something wanted that cannot be obtained without the cooperation of another person. It is an objective for which a person can assume no responsibility because it is beyond his control. Reaching a desire must never become the motivating purpose behind behavior, because then a person is assuming responsibility for something he cannot fulfill on his own.[5]

Stated very simply, a *goal* is something I want that I can control. A *desire* is something I want that I cannot control.

Wanting to lose weight is a legitimate goal because I am solely responsible for what I eat and whether I exercise. Wanting my husband to lose weight can be only a desire because I definitely cannot control his eating or exercising. I know wives who have programmed their husbands' eating, placing one very small chicken breast and two stalks of broccoli on the plate, and the response was far from positive.

I asked several wives, "What is your goal for your marriage?" Here are some responses:

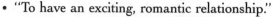

- "To have an exciting, romantic relationship."
- "To have a wonderful marriage."
- "To have my marriage be a picture of Christ's love."
- "To develop a deep intimacy in all areas of our marriage."

Each goal sounds positive, even "lofty," certainly a good goal to have. Right? Wrong! Go back to the definition of a goal. My goal for my marriage has to be something I can work toward.

Reread my personal marriage statement. Every choice was something I could control. I can seek to love, to encourage. I can do *my* part to bring about an intimate oneness.

One of the most important things to learn in life and love is that I can be responsible only for what I can control. I can control me; I can make decisions, choices, for me—*not* for my husband.

Sarah was angry and frustrated because she couldn't control her husband, Sam. He wouldn't do *his* part to bring about a wonderful openness and intimacy in their marriage. Sarah's goal—to have an intimate oneness, a close, wonderful relationship, with her husband—could be only a desire. Her deep desire and prayer could be to have an intimate oneness. Her goal could be to be a godly wife and do *her* part to bring about intimacy.

Recently, I found some notes written years ago when I was trying to discover why I was frustrated despite working so hard at being a wife and mother. Here is what I wrote in the wee hours of the morning:

My goal can only be to be a godly wife. My desire and earnest prayer—to have a wonderful marriage. I am re-

sponsible for me. I am not responsible for my husband. I can't be responsible for what I can't control and I certainly cannot control my husband. BUT I can control me or better stated, I can learn to control me. . . . I can learn, with God's power and motivation, to daily make the choices that will lead me toward my goal of being a godly wife.

So, my daughters, you *pray for desires* and *work for goals*. In the next letter, I want to share with you about our secret choices, the daily inward decisions that lead us to *live* a marriage statement.

I love you,
Mom

$\mathcal{A}$RE WE AWARE OF THE POWER OF OUR SECRET CHOICES?

Dear Joy and Robin,

When the alarm went off at six A.M., Mary Lou opened her eyes, then sank back into sleep. Her husband, Bill, made his breakfast and ate alone. Mary Lou felt rather badly about it, but the choice was simplified several mornings later when she didn't even hear the alarm. Bill began going to the Doughnut Shop for breakfast and companionship where an attractive waitress provided both.

Bill and Mary Lou had established the habit of exchanging kisses and hugs whenever one of them left the house.

But Bill, miffed at Mary Lou's failure to get up for breakfast with him, decided one morning to leave without her sleep-fogged kiss. Mary Lou, hurt when she realized what he had done, retaliated by ignoring him that evening. Both were out of sorts at bedtime and turned their backs on one another instead of exchanging good-night hugs.[6]

There are no major decisions here, but many small choices are affecting this marriage. Life is a series of choices, most of them so small we usually don't even realize that we're making them or why we're making them. Sometimes we call them *reactions* and disclaim any responsibility for them, not recognizing that reactions are choices too. I'm sure if we could talk to Bill and Mary Lou, they would be shocked to hear that their tension and distance had occurred because of their wrong choices. "What wrong choices? It just happened," they would say. Nothing in marriage "just happens." It is the result of a choice: "What is a choice? The voluntary act of selecting from two or more things that which is preferred."[7]

If we are like Bill and Mary Lou and not even aware that we are daily making choices, we need to seriously think about how we are living our lives. We choose many times every day: I will encourage my husband, I will accept, I will love, I will forgive, I will listen, or I won't . . . I won't . . . I won't. . . .

Not only are we often unaware of our choices, but we seldom give much thought about where they are taking us and whether we want to go there! Our choices may be small when counted one at a time, but their cumulative effect is more powerful than

we can imagine. Dr. Ed Wheat says, "These private choices direct our steps, determine our behavior, change the quality of our relationships and in the end shape our lives."[8]

An intimate oneness in marriage is built by the choices we make day by day. A marriage relationship is not just saying one "I do" at the wedding ceremony. Instead, the relationship is formed by the many small "I do's" and "I don'ts" each day, which become an accumulation of hundreds of thousands of "I do's" and "I don'ts."

It's like the story of a wealthy man who was concerned about the financial plight of a home builder. The rich man contracted with the builder for a house to be built on a lot he owned. He requested that nothing be spared in the quality of materials and workmanship.

The builder was grateful for the job, but he saw an opportunity to increase his profits by using inferior materials and cutting corners on the quality of craftsmanship. None of the shoddy work or cheaper materials showed, but the builder knew things were not built as they ought to have been.

When the house was completed, the generous rich man said to the builder, "I've been concerned for you and want to help you get back on your feet. That's why I had this house built. I'm giving it to you for as long as you live in it. You are now the owner, and your family can move in right away."[9]

You can imagine the astonishment and the sorrow of the builder. If he had only known, he would have built a first-class house.

As wives, we are building a relationship with our husbands, and each positive choice we make for our marriages is like an

extra nail or a reinforcing piece for a house. We build either with quality materials and excellent craftsmanship or with just enough to get by. And what we build by our secret choices into the love relationship with our men, we live with.

Each time you say, "I do" or "I don't," you make a choice, a secret choice. I say *secret* because the choices that determine the success of your marriage are made first on the inside, known only to you and God. Later, the results can be seen by all. Will you feel good about the decisions you are making today in five years, in ten years? How do you really love your man?

You must choose to love your man, or your lack of choice will head you in the opposite direction.

I love you,
Mom

2
MEETING OUR NEEDS

$\mathcal{W}$HAT ARE OUR REAL NEEDS?

Dear Daughters,

Do you remember the love relationship between Rocky and Adrian in the original *Rocky?* The big hunk and the wallflower from the pet shop were definitely an unexpected match, and Pauly, the insensitive goon and brother of Adrian, could not figure out why Rocky would be attracted to his sister. "I don't get it," Pauly said. "What's the attraction?" Do you remember Rocky's answer?

"I don't know—fills gaps, I guess."

"What's gaps?"

"She's got gaps. I got gaps. Together we fill gaps."

In a simple but profound way, Rocky hit upon a truth. He was saying that without him, Adrian had empty places in her life, and without her, he had empty places in his. But when the two of them got together, they met the needs in the other.

What are your husband's needs? What are yours? Obviously, to learn to love this unique man God has given to you, you must understand his needs! Easier said than done.

Discourses abound; lists are plentiful. The problem is, the lists don't match. The book, *His Needs, Her Needs,* by Willard F. Harley, Jr., deals exclusively with the subject. Harley states that although each individual may perceive needs differently, the following lists have consistently surfaced as he counseled thousands of couples:

Man's Five Most Basic Needs in Marriage:

1. Sexual fulfillment
2. Recreational companionship
3. An attractive spouse
4. Domestic support
5. Admiration

Woman's Five Most Basic Needs in Marriage:

1. Affection
2. Conversation
3. Honesty and openness
4. Financial support
5. Family commitment[1]

I asked your father what he thought about this list of a man's needs. His answer was that he couldn't even begin to identify with it. To him, an intimate oneness in all areas was of utmost importance. Let's try another list taken from a book about the sexual relationship.

A man needs a woman to be his:

1. Lover
2. Cheerleader

3. Mom[??!!!??]
4. Best friend
5. Animal tamer [??!!??]
6. Competent adult

A woman needs a man to be her:

1. Hero
2. Playmate
3. Friend
4. Lover[2]

There is no way to describe your father's comments about this list. After he finished laughing, he jokingly said that he had secretly always wanted me to be like a mom to him. That's definitely a hard one to figure out; if a man is out there who wants his wife to act like his mother, I haven't met him.

Obviously, the lists from just two books are very different. To understand the needs of men and women, we need to go to the Book, to the One who created us male and female, the One who created marriage, and discover *His* list of his needs, her needs. In Genesis 2, God clearly defines the two deep-felt needs of both man and woman: the need for companionship and the need for intimacy. Sylvester Stallone might have "played dumb" in the role of Rocky, but he was right about the fact that all humans have "gaps." God agrees with Rocky; He made us relational people, and we *need companionship*.

Adam, the first man, had many things in the Garden of Eden: a perfect relationship with God, a perfect environment, some-

thing to occupy his time, an infinity of things to explore. But one thing was missing: someone to walk through the Garden with, work with, laugh with, share with; someone to love. Adam seemed to have everything, but he was alone.

In the Chinese language, whole words are written with a symbol. Often two completely unlike symbols, when put together, have a meaning different from their two separate components. A beautiful example is the symbol of *man* and of *woman*. When combined, they mean *good!* And that is exactly what God said. During the creation week, the book of Genesis notes several times, "God saw that it was good." In Genesis 2:18, the first "not good" in the Bible is recorded: "Then the LORD God said, 'It is not good for the man to be alone; I will make him a helper suitable for him'" (NASB).

When God brought the woman to Adam, his response was ecstatic: "This is it!" (TLB). Today he might say, "Wow, right on! All right, that's the one!" Adam was definitely pleased with his "suitable helper." God had created for him a companion; someone to come alongside and share the challenge of life; someone who would feel as he felt, exude joy at discovery, problem solve with him in time of puzzlement.

In the same way that God created Eve to meet Adam's needs, God has brought you to your beloved to be his "suitable helper." In the English language, that term doesn't sound very exciting. Webster even defines a *helper* as "one that helps; especially a relatively unskilled worker who assists a skilled worker, usually by manual labor." Sounds like a hausfrau clothed in dreary rags scrubbing a floor.

Obviously, God did not have Webster's definition in mind. In

the Hebrew language of the Old Testament the word *helper* conveys the idea of someone who "assists another to reach complete fulfillment." God's answer to man's need was to bring one who would provide those missing pieces from the puzzle of life. A best friend.

What is a best friend? An English publication offered a prize for the best definition of a friend, and among the thousands of answers received were the following: "one who multiplies joys, divides grief"; "one who understands our silence." But the definition that won the prize was this: "the one who comes in when the whole world has gone out."[3]

God met man's and woman's need for companionship by providing a best friend, but He went beyond mere friendship when He proclaimed that the one who would be your friend would also be your lover. In this lover-best friend, your needs for intimacy would be met as you would share an incredible intimate oneness.

I love you,
Mom

*W*HAT DOES INTIMACY FEEL LIKE?

Dear Daughters,

What does intimacy look like? What does it feel like?

Paul Stevens says that we were created with a need for intimacy, but that intimacy is not something we get through having therapy sessions or by exploring another person's body. Rather, it is the fruit of a lifetime of belonging to one other person.[4] The

stage was set for intimacy when God commanded the first man to leave and cleave to his wife: "For this cause a man shall leave his father and his mother, and shall cleave to his wife; and they shall become one flesh. And the man and his wife were both naked and were not ashamed" (Gen. 2:24–25 NASB).

LEAVE When we marry, we hope to physically leave our former homes. In many cultures, the physical leaving is not a viable possibility, but there must be a transfer of allegiance. There must also be a psychological break, an attitude that says, "My husband is now my priority and not my parents."

In the Chinese culture, when a man marries, custom requires that his mother be first and his wife second. I talked to women in Hong Kong who described untold heartaches and problems because of this failure to obey God's command to leave. In our culture, often a wife does not break the habit of allegiance to the mother or father first. To truly be one flesh, you must *leave*.

CLEAVE The word literally means to "stick like glue." Having left your former home, you bond with your spouse and become one flesh. The more you cleave, the more one-fleshed you become, a physical, mental, emotional, and spiritual intimacy. Cleaving is the process, one-fleshedness the result. Mike Mason has expressed in a beautiful way what it means to cleave:

The Lord God made woman out of part of man's side and closed up the place with flesh, but in marriage He reopens this empty, aching place in man and begins the process of putting the woman back again, if not literally *in* the side, then certainly *at* it: permanently there, intrusively there, a sudden lifelong resident of a space which until that point the

man will have considered to be his own private territory, even his own body. But in marriage he will cleave to the woman, and the woman to him, the way his own flesh cleaves to his own bones.[5]

ONE FLESH   I've read many definitions of *intimacy*, but the best, most succinct, most beautiful one is recorded here in Genesis: "And the man and his wife were both naked and were not ashamed."

What does it mean to be naked? Is it only a physical condition? The first husband and wife experienced nakedness in all areas: a physical, emotional, intellectual, and spiritual transparency between husband and wife; no masks, no barriers; only communion and companionship.

They were unashamed. They enjoyed an intimacy where there was no fear to reveal, a transparency that let the other into the deep crevices of life. Neither partner feared to let the other see the good, the bad, the indifferent. They could know and be known without fear; they had no hidden agendas, no hang-ups, no embarrassments; they lacked self-consciousness.

What an indescribably beautiful provision by God! The needs for companionship and intimacy so perfectly met in a live-in lover-best friend! C. S. Lewis, in his powerful way with words, describes this intimacy experienced with his beloved wife:

We feasted on love; every mode of it, solemn and merry, romantic and realistic, sometimes as dramatic as a thunder-

storm, sometimes comfortable and unemphatic as putting on your soft slippers.

She was my pupil and my teacher, my subject and my sovereign, my trusty comrade, friend, shipmate, fellow-soldier. My mistress, but at the same time all that any man friend has ever been to me.[6]

Perhaps no one has explained the key words *leave, cleave,* and *one flesh* better than Walter Trobisch in his book *I Married You.* Trobisch helps us understand that the marriage covenant has a public part, leaving father and mother, a personal part, cleaving, and a private part, one flesh:

Leaving is symbolized by wedlock, that public act by which two people state they belong to each other in an exclusive relationship. Cleaving means the joining of two people in a friendship that will extend throughout their lives. One flesh is the fulfillment of the first two, when a couple expresses with their bodies the reality of leaving and cleaving.[7]

My daughters, your marriage ceremony is your Garden of Eden. Growing to become one flesh is a process that takes a lifetime, beginning when God declares you one. He declares it, but now you have to live it out, day by day, choice by choice. Now you begin to learn how to really love your man.

I love you,
Mom

$\mathcal{W}$HAT DO I DO WITH *MY* NEEDS?

Dear Joy and Robin,

Many marriages fail today not because people expect too little of marriage but because they expect too much. They come with an empty bowl saying, "I need security; I need affection; I need life direction; I need love and encouragement; I need an identity; I need to know who I am. I come with my empty bowl to you, for you are a wonderful person. I know you can fill it right up." But before long the partner says, "It just so happens I have an empty bowl too." So you exchange empty bowls until you realize your marriage is not based on a strong foundation.[8]

Obviously, no wife can perfectly respond and respect, and no husband can perfectly love and lead. Each of us hopes to grow year by year to be more the person the beloved needs, but we must realize that perfection on this earth will never be a reality.

What do you do as a wife when your husband doesn't fill your "empty bowl"? What do you do with your unmet needs? For years I have carried around with me the following quote by Dr. James Dobson:

> With regard to your husband, my advice is that you change that which can be altered, explain that which can be understood, teach that which can be learned, revise that which can be improved, resolve that which can be settled, and ne-

gotiate that which is open to compromise. Create the best marriage possible from the raw materials brought by two imperfect human beings with two distinctly unique personalities. But for all the rough edges which can never be smoothed and the faults which can never be eradicated, try to develop the best possible perspective and determine in your mind to accept reality exactly as it is. The first principle of mental health is to accept that which cannot be changed. You could easily go to pieces over the adverse circumstances beyond your control, but you can also resolve to withstand them. You can will to hang tough, or you can yield to cowardice. Someone wrote:

> Life can't give me joy and peace;
> it's up to me to will it.
> Life just gives me time and space;
> it's up to me to fill it.

You may have to accept the fact that your husband will never be able to meet all of your needs and aspirations. Seldom does one human being satisfy every longing and hope in the breast of another. Obviously, this coin has two sides: You can't be his perfect woman, either. He is no more equipped to resolve your entire package of emotional needs than you are to become his sexual dream machine every 24 hours. Both partners have to settle for human foibles and faults and irritability and fatigue and occasional nighttime "headaches." A good marriage is not one where perfection reigns; it is a relationship where a healthy perspective over-

looks a multitude of "unresolvables." Thank goodness my wife, Shirley, has adopted that attitude toward me![9]

God wants us to adopt this attitude toward our husbands. It is one answer to the unmet needs question. To know the final solution, you'll have to wait for my next letter.

Much love,
Mom

HOW DO WE ASSUME PERSONAL RESPONSIBILITY FOR OUR NEEDS?

Dear Daughters,

May the God who gives endurance and encouragement give you a spirit of unity among yourselves as you follow Christ Jesus, so that with one heart and mouth you may glorify the God and Father of our Lord Jesus Christ. Accept one another, then, just as Christ accepted you, in order to bring praise to God (Rom. 15:5–7).

While I was visiting my friend Michelle, she shared with me from her personal journal the story of how God had taught her what He wanted her to do with her unfulfilled needs. Because she stated so beautifully a concept sometimes difficult to grasp, I asked her if she would be willing to write her story to me in a letter so I could share it with you.

After Josh and I had been married for a couple of years, I began to feel depressed and unhappy. I think that I had married really believing in my heart (though I probably wouldn't have acknowledged it) that all my needs for love, acceptance, and security would be met in marriage. I thought I would be married to someone who would always be on my side, would adore and love me no matter what I did, and would understand me completely even when I didn't understand myself.

I began to be confused, frustrated, and angry because this wasn't happening. I thought maybe I wasn't trying hard enough, so I worked hard to do all the things for Josh that communicated love to me, like writing little love notes and buying him surprises. I tried harder and harder at losing weight, cleaning house, and memorizing facts about current events, so I would be interesting. These are not bad things, but I was not doing them for Josh. I was doing them in order to get him to do something for me, namely make me feel totally loved and secure.

When trying harder didn't work, I tried confronting him on how he wasn't loving me enough. I also tried appealing to his sympathy by crying and being pitiful. I finally concluded that Josh either would not or could not love me the way I needed to be loved.

I vividly remember the afternoon when this finally sank in. I was furious at God. I told Him that I had prayed for my mate since I was in the ninth grade. I had prayed about my engagement to Josh. I had tried to follow God every step of

the way. God, better than anyone, knew how I needed to be loved. How could He do this to me? I remember hitting my bed in anger and crying. As I sat there it became clear to me that somebody was going to have to give in this argument. It was going to be God or me, and chances were good it was going to be me.

I knew that God was asking me to change. I needed to give those needs and desires to Him as a sacrifice and trust Him to meet them, however He chose. That is easy to say, but overwhelming to actually do. I felt as if God was literally asking me to cut my heart out and give it to Him. (On top of that I had no anesthesia and I had to do the surgery myself.) To be loved and cared for the way I had dreamed in marriage was what I had lived for all my life. To me it was the meaning of life. To give up hope of having it seemed like giving up my life. It was like a death. I laid across my bed and cried and cried until I was completely exhausted both physically and emotionally.

And then it dawned on me that this is what it means in a practical way to deny myself and follow Him. This is what it means to lose my life for His sake (Matt. 16:25). I decided to write out in my journal the specific things that I was giving to God that day. These are a few of the things that were on my list:

1. The belief that my marriage would make me secure.
2. The belief that my marriage would completely fill my need for love.
3. The idea that any human being can love me completely without ever wavering.

4. The belief that my emotional maturity, my fulfillment, and happiness was Josh's responsibility.

5. The belief that Josh's emotional maturity, fulfillment, and happiness was my responsibility.

After I wrote these things out in my journal I experienced peace and joy for the first time in weeks. I was even feeling humorous. I wrote in my journal, "Now, God, is there anything else You want, as long as I have the incision open here?"

As I look back over the years since that day, I see it as a real turning point. My mission in marriage was changed from getting my needs met to letting God teach me how to love Josh, just for the sake of obeying and pleasing God. This has been really hard. Many times the decision to love is very private. There is no one to applaud or to say, "Boy, Michelle, that was really an unselfish thing to do." There is no one there who knows how much it hurts in that moment to choose to love, except God.

I have learned and I am still learning how to tell God about my needs and trust Him to meet them. He does meet them in surprising ways. I am also learning that as I love Josh without pressuring him with expectations, God has been teaching him how to better love me and meet my needs.

My daughters, Michelle said it all. Reread her letter. It takes more than one reading to digest. She has found the road to peace.

I love you,
Mom

$\mathcal{H}$OW CAN I KNOW MY MAN'S UNIQUE NEEDS?

Dear Daughters,

You have found him, your one unique man to love, an original unlike any other. You are beginning this adventure called marriage with him, and *you* are the one close to his heart who knows his deep needs. You don't have to meet the needs of any other man, only one, but it can take a lifetime to intimately know, to learn to understand, to learn to love and discover your original creation.

The more you understand your husband's uniqueness, the more you understand his deep needs, the more you can meet them. Marriage is the adventure of discovering each other so you might deeply share

- a soul intimacy.
- a body intimacy.
- a spirit intimacy.

The three intimacies together yield oneness. Sex without soul intimacy is empty, satisfying only the body. Soul and body intimacy without spirit oneness is missing God's best. God made us three-dimensional people. Man and woman are to meet body, soul, and spirit; the result will be a lover-best friend relationship.

What your husband needs will be a reflection of his longing for *companionship, intimacy,* and *significance.* How his needs will be demonstrated will be unique because he is unique. That is why, as a wife, you must make it your project to study your man. Where do you begin?

Begin by asking God. Psalm 139 declares that God understands your man's thoughts, is intimately acquainted with all his ways. The Lord is the One who can teach you all you need to know about your man. He, our Creator, was there when your man was formed and placed in his mother's womb.

Countless times I have gone to the Lord with this prayer: "Help, God. Teach me to understand this complicated man You have given me to love." Time after time, He has unraveled puzzles that I couldn't solve. Sometimes this insight has been given as I have been quiet before Him, other times through His Word or a book or the words of a friend.

How tragic that so often we go *first* to a person rather than to the One who gave our men their uniqueness. First, ask God. Second, ask your husband:

- "Honey, what is important to you in a best friend? Help me to know. Do you want me to jog with you or teach a Bible study with you?"
- "Honey, what is important to you in a lover? Tell me your dreams of all you have ever desired in a lover."
- "Honey, what can I pray for you today?"

Study your man; listen to him, talk to him, and get so bold as to ask him how he would describe his five greatest needs. One

woman asked her husband to list his needs for her, and the paper he gave her listed sex five times! His answer reflects that many men find it difficult to reveal themselves. When she convinced him that she really wanted to know, he gave her his real list.

Learning to know your unique man is an art. Learning to meet his deep needs is a skill. It is a challenge that takes a lifetime.

I love you,
Mom

$\mathscr{U}$NCONDITIONAL ACCEPTANCE: A DEEP-FELT NEED

Dear Daughters,

God makes it very clear that you are to accept your husband, and if you choose not to accept him, you are sending the message: "I don't like you as you are." A lack of acceptance will result in your (1) trying to change your husband and (2) becoming a nag. Both will have a devastating effect on you as a wife and on your marriage.

Erma Bombeck is one of my favorite authors. She has a way of exaggerating the obvious and the true just enough that we can see ourselves. In this humorous column called "Great Expectations and a Face Lift That Flopped," she details her plot to change her husband:

Want to know the thought that ran through my mind as I knelt beside my new husband on our wedding day staring into one another's eyes?

I thought, "First, we're going to let his hair grow out." I hated that burr. It made him look like a shag rug that had just been vacuumed. In a couple of months, he wouldn't look like the same man.

At the reception as I watched him with his poker-playing buddies across the room, I thought: "Say goodbye to the single life. From here on in, it's just the two of us watching sunsets and holding hands at the movies. No more tour-group dating. All that is about to change."

At dinner that night I smiled in anticipation of how his eating habits were going to change. I came from a family that considered gravy a beverage. He loved vegetables, which I considered decorative garbage. I couldn't imagine spending the rest of my life with a man who had never had dumplings for breakfast.

In the weeks that followed, I knew my work was cut out for me. He was slow and precise. This drove me crazy. I would have to figure out a way to step up the carburetor of his metabolism. Sometimes I would wait in the car for 10 or 15 minutes while he cleaned out the medicine chest and re-locked the doors. I would fix this.

His personal habits needed work. He never put the cap on a ballpoint pen in his life; it always dried out and had to be discarded. And the phone. Not only was he left-handed and hung up the phone backwards, but he had an annoying habit of answering it and talking for hours and never telling me who he was talking to or what they said. I always had to beg for gossip. But I would change all of that.

In the years that followed, I never rested. There was the

matter of his wardrobe. Winter and summer, he never packed anything away. I had to make him understand that changing clothes with the seasons was as traditional as apple pie and the buzzards returning to Hinckley, Ohio.

Then, of course, I had to make him more aggressive and to get excited over something when I got excited. That wasn't asking too much. The stubborn streak, of course, had to go. I could make him cave in by crying and saying he was insensitive to my feelings. Piece of cake.

Or was it. I told him the other night that in 35 years of dedication and perseverance he still has every mannerism, habit and personality trait that drives me crazy. I have changed absolutely nothing!

He said, "OK, so I won't wear the seersucker suit next winter."

I can't believe I'd marry a wimp!

Why do we nag and try to change our husbands? I think it goes back to the "if onlys." If only my husband were different, which often means, If only he were more like me; if only he lived life like I do, planned instead of flowed, tidied instead of slobbed.

One day I asked myself the question: Why do I make continual suggestions, ask continual questions, which my husband calls "sophisticated nagging"? Taking a good hard, honest look within at my inner motives, I saw ugliness that was not pleasant to see:

1. I like my way of living life better than my husband's way. This is *pride*.

2. I want him to change so that my life will be easier. If he is more understanding, I'll be more understood. If he is more organized, I'll feel more comfortable traveling together. This is *selfishness*.

I want my husband to change because I think that I'm *right* in my approach to life, and I'll be happier if I don't have to relate to someone so different. Ugly. When I saw these motives within, I asked God to forgive me and teach me new ways to accept, new ways to understand my man. God hates pride and selfishness; they bring dishonor to Him. God loves acceptance because it brings unity to our team and praise and glory to Him.

I love you,
Mom

WILL MY HUSBAND REMAIN THE SAME AS HE IS TODAY?

Dear Daughters,
   Remember the "blackmail picture" you took of your father at Newport Beach? Clad in swimming trunks, lounging in a beach chair near the breaking waves, he looked ready to indulge in a day of sand, sun, and surf. But your father, my unique husband, would not do anything so normal and mundane. On his lap was not a novel but his laptop computer. On his head no ordinary hat but my striped shorts looking totally ridiculous yet protecting his slightly hairless head! No wonder you and your brothers quickly

grabbed your beach towels and departed for sand uninhabited by a computer nerd.

You threatened to use the beach picture as evidence of your dad's nerdiness but never did. Instead, the thought of that beach scene sends all of us into gales of laughter whenever we think of it.

The question is: Was your father, my original man, always the type to be labeled affectionately by his children as a computer nerd or by others as an intellectual? No, no, NO! When I met your father, he was known as J Cool and was a fraternity hotdog who loved parties, liked to argue, and studied on the side. If anyone had told me he would one day be a respected theologian, a man who loved to study, even when no classes demanded it, I would have laughed!

Your husband will grow and change. The majority of men will not change as much as your father, but how exciting it is to grow along with the men God has given us! I would not trade the adventure of discovery called marriage for anything. The vows you will soon repeat require much thought: "For better or worse, for richer or poorer, in sickness and in health." Perhaps you could add, "In continual change, in constant growth, in whatever unique, exciting path God puts before you."

I feel very certain I can promise you that your husband won't wear your striped shorts on his head or use a computer on the beach. (Your father is the *only* man I know who would do that!) *But* I can promise you that your husband will change, he will grow, and he will perhaps be a very different man in ten or twenty years.

My challenge has been to daily seek God and pray, "Teach me to love him, teach me how to understand this unique man You've given me to love, teach me to accept the man he is and the man he is becoming."

Love,
Mom

3

*E*NCOURAGEMENT

ℋOW DO YOU SPELL *ENCOURAGEMENT?*

Dear Joy and Robin,

Never would we have believed the impact one short letter of encouragement would have on John! Working at the United Nations, struggling to be honest and upright when one man constantly ridiculed him, John was beyond discouragement. He was in despair, headed for the third *D,* depression.

Dad typed John a letter, telling him how much he admired him for standing strong and urging him to persevere. The letter took fifteen minutes to write, not a great commitment of time. John told Dad that the letter really encouraged him, but both of us were unprepared for the comment John's wife made six months later: "You know, I can't believe it, but when I looked through John's briefcase this week, I saw that the letter was still there. He must take it out every day at work and read it!"

Fifteen minutes of time and what an impact! Naturally, this experience caused me to think more seriously about the power of encouragement and to evaluate how I was doing as an encourager.

In Hebrews 10:24–25, we are asked to "consider how to stimulate one another to love and good deeds . . . [to encourage] one another" (NASB). First Thessalonians 5:11 tells us to "encourage one another, and build up one another" (NASB). Larry Crabb

defines *encouragement* as the kind of expression that helps some-one want to be a better Christian, even when life is rough.[1] Ap-plied specifically to a wife (that's you soon!), encouragement is the kind of expression of love that helps my husband to want to be a better Christian, man, husband to me, and father to our children. My encouragement helps him become all God desires him to be, helps develop all his potential.

The word for *encouragement* means literally to "stir up," "to pro-voke," "to incite people in a given direction." Verbal encourage-ment includes the idea of one person joining another on a journey and speaking words that urge the traveler to keep pressing on despite obstacles and fatigue.[2]

My daughters, you are about to begin the exciting journey called marriage. You and your husband will walk through life together, and that walk will include discouragement, many ob-stacles, and much fatigue—days when you both feel like giving up on life and each other!

A wife can crush or encourage her man. You more than any human being know his points of deepest need, his vulnerability, his areas of sensitivity, his hidden weakness. You also know bet-ter than anyone his potential as a man, his areas of talent, his hidden strength.

You are described as a "helpmate," a "counterpart," "the one who comes alongside of." As a wife, you must ask, How do I help? How do I come alongside? Is it to crush or to encourage? Do I use the intimate knowledge of my man to strike a blow, piercing him in his areas of weakness, or knowing his weakness, do I build him up that his strength may grow stronger?

Lisa was without a doubt the most negative person I'd met in

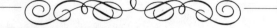

a long time. Her words were negative; she even looked negative! How can a person look negative? It's easy. What we are inside, what we continually think about, eventually shows itself in words, actions, and countenance. Kind of scary, isn't it?

Lisa had let her mind feast on gloom so long that Eeyore she became! Nothing was right. And who do you think bore the brunt of her negativism? Her husband. I watched him change from a happy-go-lucky guy to a man who looked like he held the grief of the world on his shoulders. Discouragement became his middle name, but what would you expect if the person you shared your life with tore you down, failed to see anything positive in you, and refused to encourage you as you walked through life together?

Lisa has crushed her husband, their relationship is in shambles, and neither is sure there is any love left in the marriage. It is a loveless marriage caused, I believe, by a wife's negative spirit, which grew and overflowed from thoughts to words to actions until both partners were consumed with negativism and discouragement.

Encouragement has great power, but so does discouragement. How as a wife can you grow to become the encourager God wants you to be and your husband needs? It all begins in the mind, and I'm afraid many wives need a mind transplant! (More on this in my next epistle!)

Emerson said, "Beware of what you set your mind on for that you will surely become." We want to be husband encouragers! Right thoughts lead to right words lead to right actions, and together they spell *encouragement!*

Love,
Mom

ℋOW CAN I DEVELOP RIGHT THOUGHTS?

Dear Daughters,

I ended the last letter talking about a mind transplant. You may think that is something that just moms need. How many times this past summer did I hear you say, "Mom, you've already told me that—*twice!*" Now I realize that my brain is not functioning as it once did, totally attributed I'm sure to mentalpause, as your father affectionately labels this stage of life.

However, I'm not talking about the brain, the organ God put in our heads. I'm referring to our *minds* and what we choose to dwell on. (Note once again that little word *choose.*)

"As a man thinks in his heart, so is he" (Prov. 23:7). That verse puts fear into me! It is so easy to think about nothing, to think about trivia, to think about what I don't like, about problems, about fears. If this verse is true, I could become a trivial, negative, anxious, and fearful person, just like Lisa. One man said, "There is nothing as easy as thinking, nothing as difficult as thinking right!" What is right thinking?

First, right thinking begins by controlling our thinking. Second Corinthians 10:5 instructs us to take every thought captive.

I need to be in control of my mind, not have my mind be in control of me! It's a choice I make, a conscious decision: "I *will* think about life and my husband from God's perspective and

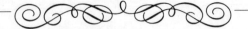

seek to encourage him." Or I can decide, "That's too hard. I'll just think about anything that happens to drift into the space between my ears." It's a difficult choice because it's *so* much easier to just let the old mind do whatever it wants.

Bill Hull in his book *Right Thinking* encourages us to have a mind transplant. That means we take out the old negative-thinking mind and allow God to implant a new mind that sees life from His perspective. Hull says the incision in this "surgery" is made by the will, and the transplant itself is performed by the Holy Spirit.[5] Paul discussed this mind-set in the book of Romans when he encouraged us to "not be conformed to this world but to be transformed by the renewing of our minds" (12:2).

Second, right thinking is setting my mind on the positive.

I can choose to dwell on the negative and be a Lisa, or I can choose to dwell on the positive and be a woman of peace. It is hard for many to name their favorite verse of Scripture. Not for me. It is imprinted on my mind and framed over the sofa in my living room so that each time I dust, I will be reminded to dwell on the positive. Philippians 4:8 has been a powerful influence in my life: "Finally, brethren, whatever is true, whatever is honorable, whatever is right, whatever is pure, whatever is lovely, whatever is of good repute, if there is any excellence and if anything worthy of praise, let your mind dwell on these things" (NASB).

I love the way Paul stated that. He was a student of human nature and knew our tendency to dwell on the negative. So he wrote, if there is *any* excellence, and if *anything* is worthy of praise, find the positive, look for it, and then dwell on it!

In verse 9 of Philippians 4, we are commanded to practice "these things" recorded in verse 8. Practice choosing to dwell on the positive and good, the lovely, gracious, excellent, and praiseworthy in your husband.

I began this letter with the verse, "As man thinks in his heart, so is he." Mom's paraphrase as applied to husbands is this: "As a wife thinks in her heart about her husband, so she will be to him." One woman wrote, "The most practical method in my own life to change my thoughts has been to memorize Scripture and to ask God to help me put His truths into practice." Planting God's Word in my heart and mind has caused the mind transplant to put down roots. I find God's perspective in God's Word. My daughters, why don't you begin now by memorizing Philippians 4:8 and applying it to the one who will soon be your husband?

Do I always follow its advice? You lived with me for many years and know the answer to that! But I keep on keeping on and meditating on this verse because each word holds such wisdom for me as a wife.

I become what I think. Right thinking leads to right words, which lead to right actions, which become encouragement to my man. It all starts in my mind but quickly comes out my mouth. I know that I need not only a mind transplant but a tongue transplant as well!

Love,
Mom

$\mathcal{I}$S WHAT I SAY REALLY SO IMPORTANT?

Dear Daughters,

A few years ago, I was involved in a Bible study where we were studying our words and their effect on other people. It was *not* one of my favorite Bible studies because after looking at all the verses in Scripture about the tongue, I felt like I needed a muzzle.

One of the projects suggested during the Bible study was to say one positive thing to our husbands and children every day for a week. I'll never forget some of the women's comments at the next lesson:

- "Those words of praise sounded so strange coming out of my lips. It must have been a long time since I had said them."
- "I didn't think the project sounded difficult. I mean, anyone could come up with one positive thing each day. But I was naive. It was very hard!"
- "I discovered that my mouth says negative words, gives instructions, and just talks without thinking. I needed this project."

Experts estimate that each of us on the average speaks enough words every day to fill at least 20 pages each day, 36 books a

year, 2,310 books in a lifetime of 65 speaking years. What a library! (I think most of us would be horrified to read the account of just one day's words.)

The purpose of this letter is to suggest not that you talk less (however, that might not be a bad idea for me!) but that you *think* about what you say and concentrate on saying positive things to your husband.

The Word of God includes the most insightful and accurate descriptions of our words and their effect on others. Husbands are included in the "others"! As I read these Scriptures, I am sobered anew at the seriousness of what we say. I think you will be sobered too:

1. *Proverbs 18:21* has only ten words, but a wife could dwell on these ten for a long time: "Death and life are in the power of the tongue." This verse is so starkly frightening that we tend to skip over it so we won't have to think about the consequences of what we say. In what way does a wife bestow life or death? Surely not in a physical sense. If words could literally kill, scores of dead people would be lying around, including many dead husbands. The death spoken of is an emotional or psychological death.

Kristi and Rob ran a business together, working closely as partners and owners of the company. How they worked together was a mystery because Kristi criticized Rob continually, in private, in public, to everyone who would listen. When Kristi discovered that she had terminal cancer, she repeatedly told Rob, "When you take over this business, you will ruin it." Rob had to deal with her death and also with the "emotional death" of her words. He pushed himself to prove that her words were false, but his fear led to alcohol, depression, and drugs. In the end, the

business, his children, and his personal life were destroyed. Kristi spoke only ten words, but they brought death.

In 1849, when Nathaniel Hawthorne was dismissed from his government job in the customs house, he went home in despair. His wife listened to his tale of woe, set pen and ink on the table, lighted the fire, put her arms around his shoulders, and said, "Now, Nathaniel, you will be able to write your novel."[4] Hawthorne did, and literature was enriched with *The Scarlet Letter*. Mrs. Hawthorne spoke only ten words, but what a difference ten of the *right* words can make! Proverbs 15:4 asserts, "A soothing tongue is a tree of life." She brought life, hope, and encouragement to her husband.

2. *Proverbs 12:18* declares,

> There is one who speaks rashly
>   like the thrusts of a sword,
> But the tongue of the wise brings healing. (NASB)

What are rash words that pierce and deeply wound our husbands? Sadly, words like these slip easily out of the mouths of wives:

- "You are so stupid. I knew I shouldn't have asked you to fix the toilet. You can't do anything right."
- "I wish I'd never married you."
- "Jane just bought a new coat. Her husband has a fantastic salary. We never seem to have enough money."
- "I wish you were different."

What are wise words that bring healing?

- "Honey, I appreciate your trying to fix the toilet."
- "I'm thankful that I married you, even though this week has been difficult."
- "I appreciate your working so hard. I know I have a lot to learn about finances."
- "I'm so thankful you are my husband!"

One day the philosopher Xanthus was expecting friends for dinner. He ordered Aesop to provide the best things for his table that the market could afford. Only tongues were provided. The cook was ordered to serve them with different sauces. Course followed course, all tongues. "Did I not order you," said Xanthus in a violent passion, "to buy the best vitals the market afforded?"

"And have I not obeyed your orders?" answered Aesop. "Is not the tongue the bond of civil society? The organ of truth and reason? The instrument of praise and adoration of the gods?"

On the morrow Xanthus ordered Aesop to go to the market again and buy the worst things he could find. Aesop again purchased nothing but tongues, which the cook was ordered to serve as before. "What—tongues again!" cried Xanthus.

"Most certainly," replied Aesop. "The tongue is surely the worst thing in the world. It is the instrument of all strife and contention, the inventor of lawsuits, the source of division and wars, it is the organ of error, lies, of slander, of blasphemy!"[5]

And we could add, it is the destroyer of human hearts, both male and female. Aesop's fable presents truth concerning both

the positive and the negative influence of our tongues. As James wrote in his epistle, "With [the tongue] we bless our God and Father, and with it we curse men, who have been made in the likeness of God. Out of the same mouth proceed blessing and cursing. My brethren, these things ought not to be so" (3:9–10).

3. *Psalm 39.* Socrates reported a story of Pambo, a plain ignorant man who went to a learned man and desired him to teach him some psalm or other. He began to read him the Thirty-ninth Psalm: "I said, I will take heed to my ways, that I sin not with my tongue." Having passed this first verse, Pambo shut the book and took his leave, saying that he would go learn that point first.

When he had been away several months, his teacher asked him when he would learn another lesson. He answered that he had not yet learned his old lesson; and he gave the very same answer to one who asked the same question forty-nine years later.[6]

Pambo was far from ignorant. He knew the tongue was more difficult to control than anything in all creation. And yet that is so necessary for us, my daughters, because it is our privilege to encourage the men God gives us and words are a big part of encouragement. As with right thinking, so with right talking. I need God's perspective on my words, that my speech might be the positive and edifying kind.

Dr. Henry H. Goddard discovered that encouragement is actually a source of fresh energy, which can be measured in the laboratory. He pioneered studies using an instrument devised to measure fatigue. When an assistant would say to the tired child at the instrument, "You're doing fine, John," the boy's energy

curve would actually soar. Discouragement and faultfinding were found to have an opposite effect, which could also be measured.[7] Here we have scientific proof that the encouragement we give our men can work miracles!

The choices we make about what we say to our men will be one of the most important decisions we make in our marriages.

I ask God to do this for me (words in brackets are Mom's additions):

> Set a guard, O LORD, [like a muzzle] over my mouth;
> Keep watch over the door of my life. (Ps. 141:3)

> Let no unwholesome [critical] word proceed from [my] mouth, but only such a word as is good for edification [building up my man] according to the need of the moment [what my man needs], that it may give grace to those who hear [that my man may be encouraged]. (Eph. 4:29 NASB)

May we be wives who learn to speak like the excellent wife in Proverbs 31:

> She opens her mouth with skillful and godly wisdom,
> And on her tongue is the law of kindness. (v. 26)

Love,
Mom

$\mathscr{H}$OW CAN OUR ACTIONS SAY "I LOVE YOU"?

Dear Joy and Robin,

I have been reading through the New Testament during the last few months, and these verses jumped out at me:

> Let us not lose heart in doing good, for in due time we shall reap if we do not grow weary. So then, while we have opportunity, let us do good to all men, and especially to those who are of the household of the faith. (Gal. 6:9–10 NASB)

> Be ready for every good work. (Titus 3:1)

> Do not grow weary in doing good. (2 Thess. 3:13)

> And let our people also learn to maintain good works, to meet urgent needs, that they may not be unfruitful. (Titus 3:14)

We are commanded to encourage others through our actions. We're instructed to be ready, to not grow weary or lose heart if people do not respond to our good work, if people do not thank us and praise us for our efforts. We are promised that in due time we shall reap.

My daughters, the *first* place to encourage with our actions is

in our homes with our husbands. Our husbands are the primary persons we are to build up, to do good to. Then, we go to others, not the reverse.

So, how do we show our love in action by deeds of encouragement?

Letters of appreciation. I have a stack of letters written over twenty-eight years of marriage by your father. Would I ever throw them away? Not on your life. I've read them and reread them. During times of discouragement, I take them out and always come away feeling uplifted that I have done something right. An anniversary is a perfect time to write the one you love telling him all you have appreciated about him during the past year, how he has grown as a husband, how his lovemaking has reached new heights, how you thank him for walking beside you during the hard times. A birthday presents another opportunity. Remember the framed letter you gave your dad on his forty-eighth birthday listing "48 Reasons Why Dad Is Great"? There were funny reasons (his cool hairstyle) but many serious reasons (because of his desire to see Christ in his children). The gift is displayed on his desk next to the picture of his four children and will probably remain there forever.

Notes. Robin, do you remember how I wrote you little notes and put them in your lunch box when you were small? You said all your friends were jealous because you got notes with stickers on them and they didn't. One mother even called me and said, "Well, I guess I have to write notes and put them in my daughter's lunch because that is all she talks about!"

What a simple thing, a few lines on a three-by-five card. Joy, I recently found a note I had written you when you were fifteen

and put on your mirror. You were trying out for cheerleading and were nervous. The note gave five reasons why you would be a good cheerleader. As a teenager, you definitely did not want stickers on your notes; in fact, you probably never mentioned receiving it, but many years later it was still in your drawer.

We are in good company when we become note writers. Abraham Lincoln was a master at encouraging others through notes. George Bush does the same. Our husbands are lifted in their spirits by notes when they are happy, when they are hurting, when they just need to be reminded that even if the rest of the world has not caught on yet, we think they are great!

When Lindsey's husband went back to school in his thirties, he was scared of keeping up with all the "young bucks." To encourage him, Lindsey made him a card every Thursday and slipped it into his lunch on Friday. The theme of her card was always, "You can do it!"; "I believe in you!"; "It's the weekend; I'll get to see more of you. I can't wait!" What a lucky man to have such a thoughtful wife, but did he ever thank her or even mention the cards of encouragement? No. For months she faithfully made his cards with never a word of thanks. (Yes, he definitely qualifies as a clod!) One Thursday when Lindsey was sick, she was unable to make her weekly card, and you guessed it, at noon on Friday, the clod called to ask her where his card was!

That brings up an interesting question. Why do we do what we do? Why do we "do good," encourage the men we love? Is it to be faithful to God and to love our men, or is it to receive praise? If Lindsey's motive had been to be thanked, she would have discontinued her card making after the first week.

Touch. Listen to one woman's description of how her husband's touch encouraged her:

> When my husband came home from work yesterday, the house was a wreck and the kids were driving me wild. When I told him I just couldn't handle it, do you know what he did? He took me to the basement, put his hands on my shoulders, looked down into my face and said very quietly, "Now just calm down." Then he put his arms around me and pulled me against him and just held me for five whole minutes without saying a word. I can't explain to you how good it felt to be in his arms like that. I began to slowly relax and escape my stressed-out world. Then he said, "Now let's take care of this and see if we can get these monsters fed and to bed early. Then we'll eat alone and be together, just you and me."

Now I call that encouragement! Don't you agree that every husband should read that wonderful account? We as wives can also through a loving touch bring warmth and encouragement to our men.

Dad's diet. Anything that our particular men need at the moment is encouragement. Recall the verse in Titus: "Maintain good works, to meet urgent needs." Throughout the years, these needs will change, and the opportunity to build up your man will be different at different times.

For me, in this twenty-ninth year of marriage, one way I can encourage my husband is to make delicacies that do not damage

arteries. My challenge has been to embellish blandness. Butter, sour cream, cream of mushroom soup, and cheese are the zest adders to food. The question is: How can a skinless chicken breast taste good without the zest adders? There is life after butter! It is possible to create tempting, tasteful meals that are not blah. It's been an adventure, and your father says he is encouraged to stay on his diet. He even made the remarkable comment that he likes eating this way and told me my homemade bread (only one fat gram per slice) was the second-best thing about me (I'm not telling his view of the first).

Your husband will probably not need a fat-free diet, at least not for many years, but as you observe your man, as you think right, talk right, and seek to act right, God will show you how *encouragement* is spelled for your unique man.

As I think back on my marriage, my heart is flooded with thankfulness for how my husband has encouraged me. Let me close this long epistle by sharing some of the ways with you:

1. As a Christian. He has encouraged me in my walk with the Lord and he has pointed me to God during dark times.
2. As a person. Your dad has helped me use my gifts and abilities. I wrote *Creative Counterpart* because he kept telling me I had a message and could do it. He outlined the book for me since outlining is definitely not my strong point. He stayed home and baby-sat for you kids while I traveled on weekends and spoke at retreats.
3. As a mother. When I was exhausted with three little ones, he sat me down one day and said, "Let's make a list of everything you feel responsible for." There were seventy-

five things on the list! "No wonder you are tired!" he said. His decision was to come home each day and ask me what I had not accomplished that was on my list. He committed to do whatever still needed to be done. He scrubbed toilets and mopped floors; he did anything.

4. As a wife. His words of praise, his letters, his praise before you children all have been great encouragements to me. The biggest sin in our home was to be disrespectful to Mommy.

5. By sacrificing for me and for you. We moved to a different location so as teenagers you could be in a more positive environment.

All of these right actions of your father that brought great encouragement to me started with a right choice followed by right thinking, which led to right words and actions, which enriched my life and caused me to want to be more of the wife my man needed and God wanted me to be. The question for us, my daughters, is this: How can we "do good" to our men today?

Love,
Mom

DO MEN NEED ENCOURAGEMENT SEXUALLY?

Dear Joy and Robin,

Our men need encouragement in all areas, but especially in the sexual area where they are most vulnerable. I can just hear

you now: "Mom, men are not sensitive about sex. We are!" You're wrong, my daughters. Men are much more vulnerable and sensitive about sex than women, and there is a reason.

God made every woman so that in many ways our bodies continually affirm our femininity to us. Every month we are reminded that we are women. (How often have you said that you could do without that reminder!) We carry children and watch our bodies change; we feel the kicking of our babies; miraculously, we are equipped to provide all our babies' needs. Truly, a mother's milk is as great a miracle as the manna God provided the Israelites in the wilderness. We're just used to the idea of nursing so it's no big deal.

The monthly period (even cramps), the kicking baby, the "basketball" figure, the sweet sounds a baby makes while nursing at a mother's breast—they all shout to us, "You are feminine. You are a woman."

What has God given a man to affirm his masculinity to him? Only one thing: the act of intercourse. His changing body, his erection, and the "taking" of his wife are his message: "You are masculine. You are a man."

When we grasp this idea, we can understand how three things might happen if a wife does not affirm a husband's sexuality:

1. A husband may retreat if discouraged in his lovemaking. If put down, just put up with, compared to other men, or ridiculed sexually, a man will distance himself from the woman who has attacked his masculinity. Devastating consequences will follow and will affect the whole marriage relationship.

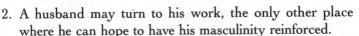

2. A husband may turn to his work, the only other place where he can hope to have his masculinity reinforced.

3. If the husband retreats, his wife may turn to her children and ignore her husband because her feminine need for affirmation is satisfied in "mothering."

Surely, the woman who wrote "Dear Abby" and said that she read during the sex act would qualify as the chief husband emasculator! But what about the woman who told me that while she and her husband were having intercourse, she said to him, "Are you about through?" (I guess *they* were not having intercourse.) I call this discouragement, separating her man from courage and confidence and good feelings about himself as a man.

A savvy woman told me, "One reason our physical relationship is so good is that I've never said anything negative about his physique or technique. I praised him (he was a good lover), but he's become even better. It's as if he's trying to live up to what I've encouraged him he is." She must have read Goethe: "If you treat a man as he is, he will stay as he is. But if you treat him as if he were what he ought to be, and could be, he will become that bigger and better man."

I can hear you wailing, "But, Mom, isn't that fake to encourage him sexually if you really don't like certain things about his loving?" Sure, it's fake if you tell untruths, and yes, you should discuss and communicate openly about your sex life. But . . . there is a way to say it and a way not to. Remember the verse that spoke of rash words that thrust like a sword or wise words that bring healing? Perhaps the way your husband touches your breasts irritates instead of excites you. You might rashly say,

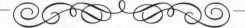

"Ouch, that hurts me. Can't you be more gentle?" Or you might speak the wise words: "Honey, I like you to play with my breasts. Could you play more gently because that gives me even greater pleasure."

Tonight I came up with a new definition of love: *Love is silence when your words might hurt. Love is praise when your words might help.*

Before I close this letter, let me remind you once again: our men, my man and your man, need encouragement, and we are in the perfect place to give it because we walk through life with them, sharing all their joys and sorrows. Today, begin with me to learn more about having *right thoughts, right words,* and *right actions,* which together spell encouragement.

I love you,
Mom

P.S. Your dad gets home from Siberia tomorrow. I'm ready to be more of an encourager!

4

COMMUNICATION

QUICK TO HEAR

Dear Daughters,

An ad in a Kansas newspaper said, "I will listen to you talk without comment for thirty minutes for $5.00." Would you believe that phone calls poured in from all over the country in answer to that ad? Ten to twenty people called every day, people willing to pay the fee plus the phone bill just so someone would listen. Listening is a lost art, but one every wife needs to find! James 1:19 makes it very clear what we need to do: "But let everyone be quick to hear, slow to speak and slow to anger; for the anger of man does not achieve the righteousness of God" (NASB).

This verse makes me feel uncomfortable inside. It doesn't sound right because it's oh, so much easier to be slow to hear, quick to speak, and quick to anger. James certainly knew where to put his "quicks" and "slows"! This is one of those verses I don't want to think about because I know I still have a long way to go before I really learn the art of listening. I'm convinced that if we as wives would apply just this one verse, the atmosphere in our homes would be very different. Let's look at it piece by piece, starting with the phrase "quick to hear."

What a creative way to say *listen!* Listening is not our natural preference. Most of us would rather be the one speaking. One man has said that the most vital communication skill in marriage

is to listen intently *with your mouth shut!* Because we would rather talk than listen, often we listen with our mouths half open, ready to insert our prized tidbit the moment our husbands take a breath!

The book of Proverbs states it another way:

> [She] who answers a matter before [she] hears it,
> It is folly and shame to [her]. (18:13)

The problem is that although many of us took courses in high school or college to help us learn to speak, no courses were given to help us learn to listen. Listening is supposed to come naturally, but it doesn't. It is a learned art, and one we must cultivate. How can we love our men unless we are quick to hear what they say, feel, believe? How can we enter into their lives without developing the gift of being quick to hear?

As I write these words, they seem inadequate to impress on you the seriousness of a simple thing like listening so I will let the words of Melissa Sands, founder of Mistresses Anonymous, speak:

> Ask any mistress. Her man doesn't do anything but talk endlessly. Mistresses are experts in the art of listening. People think a mistress has a sexual manual that keeps men bewitched, but actually what she really has is the capacity to listen.
>
> Men have mistresses because they have needs that they are unable to fill in their other lives. By needs, I mean needs to communicate—sexually, verbally, tactilely.

They don't get these needs filled at home because they see their wives when they are tired or worried about money, or early in the morning when both are at their worst, at all the wrong times.

Mistresses, however, see their men when they are at the peak of their day in energy and motivation. A married woman makes time for her job, her kids, the PTA, even her mother-in-law, but she does not make a special time for her husband. The mistress does.[1]

I know, you are gulping as I was when I first read this profound insight from the mouth of a mistress. Volumes have been written about listening, but perhaps it is really all summed up in the little phrase, "Be quick to hear." I have two suggestions to help you learn to be quick.

1. Listening effectively means that when your dearly beloved is talking, you are not thinking about what you are going to say when he stops.
2. Listening is more than politely waiting for your turn to speak. It is more than hearing the words. Real listening is receiving and accepting what your beloved is saying *plus* seeking to understand what he really means. When this happens, you can go beyond saying, "I hear your words." You can say, "I hear your heart."[2]

The ancient philosopher Zeno once said, "We have two ears and one mouth, therefore we should listen twice as much as we speak." A wife who follows this advice will not only be obeying

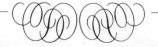

God's command to be quick to hear but will be coming one step closer to really loving her man.

I love you,
Mom

ʃLOW TO ANGER

Dear Daughters,

As we've looked together at the verse, "Be quick to hear, slow to speak, and slow to anger," I hope you have committed it to memory. It's short and to the point, easy to remember and so difficult to do.

How is it possible to be slow to anger? Anger just happens. It's just there. Your husband walks in the door and rudely says, "Oh, no, are we having tuna casserole again?" Because you are an adult, you reject the idea of throwing the hot dish in his face. Adults don't *do* childish things like that; we express our anger in much more sophisticated ways. We use our words, which can hurt far more than a hot dish. At least we can duck for cover when something is thrown at us; we can't duck words.

The response that rises naturally in you when he hurts you is probably something like this: "How dare you criticize the way I cook? At least I work hard. All you do is lie around and watch TV. If you'd gotten that raise, I could cook sirloin steak every night."

Our natural response when we are attacked is to return an insult in anger. Perhaps we didn't know the anger was even there, but our husbands make a comment and the anger just

erupts. Before we know what has happened, we have been a "quick-tempered [wife who] acts foolishly" (Prov. 14:17).

I remember getting so exasperated when you children misbe-haved when you were small. I knew I couldn't discipline you until I was under control myself. My retreat was the bathroom. I would go in, lock the door, count to ten, and then pray, "Dear Lord, this child makes me so mad. Please give me wisdom. I confess my anger. Keep me from saying what I want to say. Calm my spirit, my mind. Get my eyes off myself, my tiredness, my fear of not knowing what to do, and help me to do what is best for this child."

As I prayed, you were usually knocking on the bathroom door, "Mommy, what are you doing?" Removing myself from the scene helped me to be slow to anger. One day I realized, "Linda, you leave the scene and get your anger under control before you talk to your child. Why don't you do that with this man you love?"

I can just hear you saying, "Well, Mom, what do I do with my anger? Does God expect me to just be a stoic and always stuff it and be silent?" Definitely not. We are instructed to speak "the truth in *love*" (Eph. 4:15, emphasis added). Our problem usually isn't speaking the truth but speaking the truth *in love*.

The hope is that communication between lovers will lead to transparency. You must communicate what your husband is do-ing that hurts you, irritates you, and drives you to distraction; you must do it not in anger but in a loving way. The first step in learning to do this is to remove yourself from the scene when you are angry and "be quick to hear, slow to speak and slow to an-ger."

The second step is to learn to express your thoughts, feelings, and ideas to your husband using "I" messages instead of "you" messages:

I messages are sentences about how I am feeling or reacting to an event or communication in contrast to you-messages, which communicate an evaluation of you for your actions.

An I message communicates the effect of my spouse's actions or words on me (taking responsibility for honesty about my feelings) rather than how I think my spouse ought to change to please me (taking responsibility for his behavior). The focus of I messages is not on my spouse's sin ("You sure didn't act like much of a Christian tonight") but on how that sin has affected me ("I needed you to be there for me, and I was hurt when you weren't").[3]

Let's go back to the husband who criticized the tuna casserole. The loving wife's retort was to say, "How dare *you*," and proceed to criticize him in return. An effective message might have been this: "I feel hurt and angry when you criticize what I'm cooking for dinner because I really do try to cook what you'll like."

Sometimes it may be necessary to get control of your initial emotions before you can respond this way to your husband. I do better giving I messages if I first leave the scene, pray, make a decision to be slow to anger and *later*, when there is time alone without interruptions, express my honest feelings in love.

The natural way is to be quick to anger; it feels good to get it off your chest. The supernatural way is to be slow to anger, to wait on God for the right time and the right way to express your-

self honestly in love. Obeying God is never easy, but communicating God's way opens the way to transparency.

I love you,
Mom

$\mathcal{T}$IME TOGETHER

Dear Daughters,

Recently, I read an incredible statistic. A psychologist ran an experiment measuring the amount of conversation that occurs between the average wife and husband in a week's time. To make the experiment accurate, the researcher strapped portable electronic microphones to the subjects and measured every word they uttered: idle conversation while driving to the store; questions like, "What's in the mail?"; requests to pass the salt; everything.

There are 168 hours in a week, 10,080 minutes. How much of that time do you think the average couple devote to talking to each other? Not 7 hours, not a single hour, not even 30 minutes. On the average, the weekly conversation between husbands and wives took a grand total of 17 minutes![4]

Unbelievable! A lover-best friend intimacy cannot grow without time to talk. One man said that the central reason for being married was to enjoy and share the privilege of being vulnerable, of sharing and giving yourself to someone and inviting that person to do the same. It's impossible to develop vulnerability in two and a half minutes a day!

Deep communication cannot be scheduled. Often the most

significant conversations are not planned but spontaneous. One woman remarked that she and her husband decided to get away for an afternoon and talk. They created the time, the place, and the privacy. But the conversation just didn't take off, and she didn't know why. The conditions for a deep sharing time just aren't definable. We can make sure only that we are allowing enough opportunities for sharing to happen spontaneously.

Your dad's and my life has been as hectic as any couple's, so how did we find this scheduled time to be spontaneous?

Tea for two. I remember when all of you kids were small, trying to find time with my man. He would come in the door at night tired and needing to relax. Several little people would immediately pounce on him demanding that he play Cookie Monster with them. In desperation, we instigated Time Out for Tea, fifteen to thirty minutes when Daddy first arrived home so that he could relax with a cool glass of iced tea and me. All people under four-feet high were sent to the playroom, knowing that when teatime was over, Daddy would be theirs. Was it possible to converse in depth in fifteen minutes? Of course not, especially when you would peek around the corner and say, "Is it our turn now?" Did we have our time-out every day? Of course not. Life never fits perfectly into our plans, but planning tea for two meant we often grabbed the minutes together. Sometimes we talked very little, but just enjoyed being together. Sometimes we exchanged information about our days, discussed problems, decided how to discipline the ones waiting in the playroom. Sometimes, the magic of intimacy was present in that small block of time, and a sharing of hearts and souls began that continued long after you children were in bed.

Deep communication will *not* always just happen, but it will happen much more often if we are together frequently. Dating your mate fosters communication, creating the atmosphere where both can unwind and open up and share. While I am writing you these letters, our good friends Dave and Claudia Arp are writing the book *52 Ways to Date Your Mate* (Nashville: Thomas Nelson, 1992). Be sure to read it because it will be full of creative tips.

Escape together. Get away for six hours, one night, a weekend or, if possible, longer! When you were small, it was hard to escape for long periods of time so your dad and I would take mini-escapes. Leaving at 5:00 or 6:00 P.M., we would drive to a motel six blocks away from where you played with the baby-sitter. We had a picnic basket full of goodies, a tablecloth, candles, a tape recorder with soft music, and six hours to laugh, love, and share. I still remember the transparency, the beautiful openness in that rather old little room. I remember, too, feeling like we were doing something rather risqué as we crept out of the room at midnight, picnic basket in tow, and drove the short distance home. I told my man that next time we were going farther away from home. He laughed when I said someone who knew us had probably been walking the dog at midnight and the rumors would be, "Missionaries seen leaving motel at 12:00 A.M.!"

Are you shocked, my daughters, that your old parents would do such crazy things? I hope you will be just as crazy. A neighbor once asked me what in the world we did when we went away for the weekend. Her attitude was that married couples are to be stodgy, dull, and routine. God forbid! Sadly, her marriage ended in divorce. I grieved when she said, "Now I understand why you

went away," but it was too late for them to laugh, love, and listen.

The mistress I quoted said that men have mistresses because they have needs that they are unable to fill in their other lives. By needs, she meant the need to communicate sexually, verbally, and tactilely. On our six-hour escape date, we were able to communicate in all ways. The date cost less than going out to dinner and a movie. I'm sure the mistress is right about a man's needs, but I, too, need to communicate sexually, verbally, and tactilely. We all do.

Much love,
Mom

$\mathscr{P}$RAY, PLAN, AND PERSEVERE

Dear Daughters,

This week I talked with a young woman and encouraged her to escape with her husband. For fifteen minutes she bent my ear with a myriad of reasons why it just wasn't possible for them to escape. I told her that if they couldn't find the time *now,* the odds were, they would never find it. Unless you're of the jet set with unlimited funds, few responsibilities, and a flexible work schedule, escaping together will not happen naturally. You will need to practice the three *p* words: *pray, plan,* and *persevere.*

Why do I say *pray?* Your relationship is of great importance to the Lord, and He cares about every aspect of it. I'll never forget praying in a meeting in Romania about the women's sexual relationship with their husbands. Later, one woman said, "No one has ever prayed about such a thing before, but it was good. I

think we should pray about these things." We should also pray about time to communicate, time to be alone to be lovers and best friends.

Why do I say *plan?* Because the pressures of life and the needs of other people automatically seem to take precedence over our oneness. We'll be alone "later," we'll escape "another time," but later and another time never come. Right now, in the newness of marriage before little feet are pattering around, you will (if you look) find time to spontaneously be together. But soon, oh, so soon, invaders will push the best aside, and only persistent planning will arrange time for each other.

Why do I say *persevere?* One dear young woman in exasperation said to me, "Forget it. It's just not worth it. After I've called the fifth baby-sitter, I just want to give up."

I could write pages of all the ridiculous, irritating, sad things that have happened to keep us from escaping together. Even after praying and planning, it seems someone is against us being alone, working to keep us in the pressure cooker of life with no time to bask in each other's love. That "someone" is Satan. I've visualized Satan's discussions with his demons and think they must go something like this:

Now dear demon, you know this couple, Jody and Linda. They want to be alone to nurture their relationship: to talk, to share, even to listen to each other. They take this to extremes, even pray and plan! Most fall more easily to our devious tactics, but these two even talk about persevering! When the babysitter got sick, the car broke down, the unexpected company arrived, and the money saved for a week-

end away went to doctor's bills, they kept trying to persevere. We can't have them communicating with warm companionship and ecstatic loving. Just think of how their Christian marriage will look. Others will want what they have! This cannot be. You must be more creative, dear demon. Think of a catastrophic technique that will break down their desire so they will give up.

Thus, the Dillow flood occurred just as we were preparing to leave for a five-day celebration of our thirteenth anniversary in the Arkansas mountains. I had visions of deep communication and romantic walks by the river. It was going to be wonderful. All of you children were parceled out at friends' houses, and I had gone to the store to get a few last-minute things. While I was gone, your father tried to fix the leak in the bathroom, but instead of the drip diminishing, it turned into a gush, which became a flood.

Returning home from the store, I found water everywhere and neighbors with buckets and mops, madly trying to get the water out of the carpeting. It was a nightmare!

Instead of going on a romantic walk by the river, I vacuumed carpets with a water vacuum, pulled carpets up and hung them over the fence, and emptied our water bed of water so we could get the water-soaked carpet out from under the bed and over the fence to drip-dry. The final blow fell when we were moving all the furniture in the bedroom. My wedding ring, which had been on the dresser, got lost. It was my anniversary, and I didn't even have a wedding ring!

So, instead of going on a romantic walk by the river, I walked

around the house with tears streaming down my face, flashlight in hand, looking in every nook and cranny for my ring, but no ring was to be found. Finally, we found a bed that was still standing and slept the sleep of the exhausted. Early the next morning, I was planning my day: first the ring, then the house and the carpets. Before I could put my planning into action, my husband made an incredible statement, the kind only a man could make: "Honey, let's just forget all this mess, bring the carpets in off the fence, pile them in the living room, and head for the mountains. We still have four days left of our trip." I looked at the water-logged house and then in amazement at my man; he really meant it! How could I just leave it all and forget it? The last thing I wanted at that point was a romantic walk by the river. I wanted to find my wedding ring and try to salvage my carpets.

My feelings were screaming, "No, you can't go," so I took my feelings and my will to the bathroom, locked the door, sat on the closed potty, and prayed, "Lord, You know how I feel. I don't want to be alone with my husband. All I can think about is my stale-smelling house and my wrinkled carpets. But, Lord, my husband has said, 'Let's go,' and I know he's right. There will always be a reason why it's not a good time to escape. This time the reason just seems *very big,* but I choose in my will to go with my husband, I choose to forget the mess, and I trust You to change my feelings."

I remember that five-hour ride to the Arkansas mountains like it was yesterday. In reality, it was fifteen years ago. It remains so clear in my memory because it was a five-hour battle between my feelings and my will. Every ten minutes I would start to think about my lost ring, the soggy carpets, and the mess, and I would

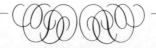

have to choose to reject the thoughts and concentrate on my husband. Gradually, and I do mean gradually, my feelings went along with the choices in my will.

By the time we arrived at our hideaway, we had three days left together. How do I describe those thirty-six hours? There truly are no words to relate the beautiful intimacy that we experienced. The depth of our communication reached a new level, we sensed a more profound oneness between us, and we even had a romantic walk by the river!

I have always believed that God rewarded me with those beautiful hours because I made a *secret choice* to make my relationship with my man a priority when it was very difficult to do.

Three key words: *pray, plan,* and *persevere.* I am not telling you that it is easy to live these three *p*'s; I am telling you that it is so worth it! Why not begin today to plan an escape with your man?

I love you,
Mom

P.S. Seven years after the notorious Dillow flood, the people living in our house found my wedding ring. Your father saved it and gave it to me on our twentieth anniversary.

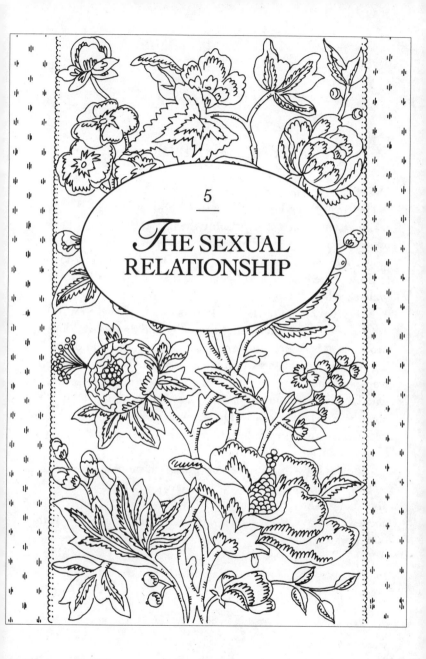

5

THE SEXUAL RELATIONSHIP

$\mathcal{D}$ID THIS REALLY HAPPEN?

Dear Daughters,

Have you ever been told a story and wondered if it could really be true or if it was possibly the figment of someone's lively imagination? This story caused me to wonder, but I have been assured that it actually happened. The names have been changed to protect the innocent and guilty, and as you read the story, you will see why!

Every young couple in love knows that it is hard to wait until marriage to enjoy each other sexually, and as the wedding approaches, it becomes more and more difficult. Jacki and Jon had trained themselves to restrain themselves and were determined to wait until they were married. They wanted to obey God. They wanted His best, but *it was not easy!* People didn't help: "You mean you're both virgins? That's awful. Your honeymoon won't be any fun. You should sleep together now so you can enjoy your honeymoon."

Motivated by this advice and finding it more and more difficult to *not* fully express their love, Jacki and Jon decided to go ahead and take the plunge. Jacki lived with her parents, so they chose a time when everyone was away from home. When they had progressed to the "sans clothing" stage, the phone rang. Jacki rolled her eyes as she heard her mother's voice and answered, yes, she would go downstairs to turn off the iron her

mother had left on. Feeling very dramatic, Jon laughingly picked up his naked fiancée and carried her down the stairs. Halfway down, he tripped, and Jacki ended up at the bottom of the stairs with a broken leg. As Jon rushed to her side, relatives and friends burst in the door shouting, "Surprise! We're having a party for you! We called and asked you to turn off the iron to be sure you were home!"

You can guess who was surprised. How do you explain to everyone that you really haven't "done it" yet and the only reason you are naked together at the bottom of the stairs is that you were afraid sex was going to be such a scary deal, you had to perform just right and you didn't want your honeymoon ruined. Would you believe that?

Jacki walked down the aisle a few weeks later with a cast on her leg. Today she and Jon can laugh about the experience. They say when they are asked their most embarrassing moment, they don't have to think twice. But can they tell anyone about the experience?

The story is true. It was humiliating. But the sad thing to me is that Jacki and Jon felt so pressured about sex. Every young couple will feel pressure to have sex, but how sad that they felt so afraid of God's gift. Has our society so indoctrinated us through the fantasy machines of movies and television that Christian young people are afraid to wait for marriage and enjoy the fun and adventure of discovery without instant perfection? I can assure you that the rewards of waiting are well worth the frustration. The wedding night is only the beginning of a lifetime of growing together in the intimacy of sexual love.

Love,
Mom

ℛEALITY VS. THE MOVIES: WHICH IS TRUE?

Dear Daughters,

From the myriad images of artificial loving, a cunning message comes through. The message is fake, but it speaks loudly. Here is what we see in the movies:

1. Sex always just happens naturally.
2. The woman is always instantly passionate, instantly ready.
3. She never needs love, encouragement, or foreplay. Her sexual glands are always active.
4. Both the man and the woman know everything, do everything just right, and are instant perfect lovers.
5. Neither the man nor the woman ever has morning breath. It's as if they have always just brushed.

Reality is reality. Movies and television are not reality, but their message about the sexual relationship has spoken loudly. One young wife said to me, "In the movies it looks so simple. I feel like there is something wrong with me. I need foreplay, time to be aroused sexually. How can women be instantly passionate? Is there something wrong with me?"

Another new bride said, "I guess I'm just not a very passionate person. Sometimes when we make love, I have something on my mind about work, our apartment, etc., and it is really hard for me to get into lovemaking. I feel like there must be something wrong with me."

There is something wrong but not with these wives. The "wrongness" is in the media message blaring across our country. We see it on screen; we read it in magazines and books; it is broadcast loudly to all our senses. It is not only wrong, it is artificial, and even worse, it is from the pit. Yes, I mean Satan's pit. Satan, the deceiver, whose purpose and plot is to present a counterfeit picture of God's perfect plan.

In the beginning God said, "The two shall be one flesh." The reference is to total oneness, a coming together of body, soul, and spirit. This oneness is made complete with the ecstasy of an intimate sexual relationship. In God's plan there is reality because real people are involved. Here is what life is like for these people:

1. Sex does not always just happen. In reality telephones ring, babies cry, and people get tired.
2. The wife is not always instantly passionate, instantly ready.
3. The wife does need love, encouragement, and foreplay; her sexual glands need activating.
4. Neither the husband nor the wife knows everything. Loving takes learning. It takes time. That's part of the fun of growing in oneness! If it all happened instantly, half the excitement of discovery would be lost!

In the Old Testament we read, "When a man takes a new wife, he shall not go out with the army, nor be charged with any duty; he shall be free at home one year and shall give happiness to his

wife whom he has taken" (Deut. 24:5 NASB). Dr. Howard Hendricks notes that in the Hebrew, the meaning of "shall give happiness to his wife" means to give sexual pleasure!

What unique ideas God has! In reality, a couple should concentrate on learning to pleasure each other for one year. How much more exciting than instant superficiality!

Your dad and I decided that if God thought it was a good idea for one year, why not continue learning to love every year! And every year has gotten better! The American myth is that sex is for the young and the beautiful but will obviously fade as you grow older. I remember when I'd been married five years. I talked with a woman who said, "Just wait, you'll find out. Sex gets old. Wait until you've been married twenty years." Well, I've been married almost thirty years, and she was wrong!

Relationships do not fit into an instant format. There is no microwave marriage manual. Nothing in marriage will happen instantly. A deep, abiding, growing intimate oneness takes work, hard work, but oh, it is so worth it! God's plan, not the movies, is reality, and even though in reality both husband and wife have morning breath, God's reality can be *wonderful!*

Love,
Mom

$\mathcal{I}$SN'T LOVING WHAT SEX IS ALL ABOUT?

Dear Daughters,
Back in the Ice Age, eons ago when your mother got married, young women were encouraged to realize the importance of a

woman having an orgasm. "Don't settle for less" was the message. "You deserve the very best. A woman is a full partner in sex, not a passive observer."

Did women need this advice? Yes! One friend of mine was married several years before she experienced an orgasm; she didn't really know what it meant to reach a climax or that a woman could or should! How pleasantly surprised she was!

Today, almost thirty years later, women have been told in both Christian and secular publications, complete with diagrams of the phases or orgasm, how to have an orgasm, what you do, don't do, ad nauseam. Of course, much of the description has been helpful to many, but is it possible that amid the pages of elaborate details of what will hopefully happen physically, the mysterious excitement of discovery has been lost? Instead of two lovers loving each other, two programmers try to follow the program, plugging the right commands into their personal body computers, and the printout reads multiorgasmic ecstasy! Yes, women can be multiorgasmic; yes, that is good; yes, ecstasy is what God wants for you and your husband. The book of Proverbs tells you to intoxicate your husband with delight and to always enjoy the ecstasy of your love!

And yes, you need all the information. Just remember, sex is *the* most intimate way of loving your man. Yes, you love him when you cook his favorite meal, listen, care about his cares, rejoice with him, cry with him, and pray for him. But the most intimate loving is when you love him physically, when you seek to express your deep commitment and love to each other by pleasuring each other beyond your wildest dreams.

Recently, I counseled a new bride. Sex had been by far her

most difficult adjustment in marriage. The formula was not producing the desired results. I asked her if she could concentrate on just seeking to love her new husband and on being loved by him and not on pushing the appropriate buttons. My question was a revelation to her. But after all, isn't loving what sex is all about?

Becoming "one flesh" is a beautiful process, so consider these points:

1. Be informed. Read (I'll list some good books at the end of this letter), discuss all with your man, and try to understand the diagrams.
2. Then concentrate on loving your man, not on the information.

I love you,
Mom

Mom's List of Good "Sex Books":

1. The Bible—best information on sex ever written
2. *Solomon on Sex* by my favorite author (your father)
3. *The Gift of Sex* by Clifford and Joyce Penner
4. *Intended for Pleasure* by Ed and Gaye Wheat
5. *For Lovers Only* by Stephen and Judith Schwambach

P.S. Do not read books two to five until one month before the wedding! You *can* read the Bible now.

*H*AS AMERICAN SEXUALITY GONE BERSERK?

Dear Daughters,

Being that I'm very close to fifty and not totally in touch with all the younger generation is thinking, I decided to buy some women's magazines to get more in tune with the thought patterns of the nineties and see just how far the world has strayed from God's perspective. After discussions with several young women, I had become discouraged because it seemed that Jacki and Jon were not the only Christians to be deceived by the media. After perusing several articles on sex, I decided that the artificial American sexuality has gone berserk! For many, the sexual relationship seems to have become a climax contest.

As one woman stated, "Sex shouldn't be a competitive sport." Her husband, having heard that a woman could be multiorgasmic, made it his mission to be sure his wife had her share! "Most of the time I experience an orgasm," she said, "but he would be disappointed if I didn't have another and yet another orgasm, so I fake it because it pleases him."[1]

Is this an isolated incident? When Abigail Van Buren, author of the "Dear Abby" column, asked women to write to tell her if they faked orgasm, she was overwhelmed by the huge volume of mail she received. Here are just a few excerpts:

Dear Abby:

Of course I fake it. All women do. I adore my husband, but he couldn't find my erogenous zone with a road map, so I go through the motions to keep from hurting his masculine ego.

Deserves An Academy Award.

Dear Abby:

I fake it just to get it over with. Sex never was as important to me as it is to my husband—but it's so good for his ego. I'd never let on that all my wild carryings on was an act. We've been married for 44 years. He's faithful and so am I, and ours is a loving, solid marriage.

Canadian Faker

Dear Abby:

Married for 22 years. Been faking it for 20.

Chattanooga Actress

Dear Abby:

I simply submit to sex as my wifely obligation to "service" my lusty husband. To him, sex is just another bodily function. I always leave the lights on so I can read something until he's finished.

Submitting Not Faking

Dear Abby:

I am a 55-year-old woman and have been married twice, and I'm not sure I've ever experienced an orgasm. Oh, I may have had one once when I was 17, and I was so overcome, I nearly blacked out. It's just as well it never happened again.

Marie In Madison[2]

Some of these comments are pathetic (like those of the woman who read during the entire sex act), but others faked orgasm for altruistic reasons (it makes my husband feel masculine). The sad thing to me is that because of the overemphasis on performance, these women felt they had to perform and to produce orgasms, if not real, then fake. I am convinced that with good communication (we'll discuss that in another letter), acting would not have been necessary.

Since I've used women's statements about orgasm to show where the new modern sexuality has taken us, and since we're on the subject, let me make a few comments about orgasm:

1. Orgasm for a wife is a very good and necessary thing.
2. Orgasm does not always happen for a woman during intercourse, the time her husband is inside her. For some women it does; for others it doesn't. For most it takes direct clitoral stimulation outside of intercourse for a wife to achieve orgasm.
3. Many couples find that it is good for a husband to bring his wife to an orgasm by other means and then enter her.

4. There is nothing sacred about a couple experiencing orgasm at the same time. It is wonderful when it happens but also very special when you can really concentrate on your husband and his enjoyment. To experience an orgasm, a wife has to concentrate on herself and what she is feeling. That is not selfish. Your response excites your husband and brings him pleasure.

5. You don't always have to engage in the act of intercourse to experience orgasm. One young woman who was pregnant told me she and her husband were uptight because for one month before the birth of the baby and one month afterward, they could not have sexual relations. I asked her why when it is very possible to love each other and satisfy each other without the husband ever entering his wife. She was concerned that experiencing an orgasm without intercourse was displeasing to God. I told her that there was nothing in the Bible to indicate that. It is perfectly proper for a husband to bring his wife to an orgasm during foreplay.

6. Often, the harder you search for release in orgasm, the more it eludes you. One young bride said she wanted so much to experience an orgasm, and of course, her husband also desired it. "I knew I just had to 'hang in there' and discover how to love my new husband and concentrate on loving and not performing. I had to allow myself to just feel and to learn how my body works, how the tension builds up. I was excited about experiencing an orgasm but knew it couldn't be my goal, and my strategy worked!"

I hope you're not shocked that your mom is being so specific about sexual issues. One of my young friends said, "Linda, why won't the Christian books answer the questions we have? I always look for answers to questions I can't ask out loud, but the books are silent." So, I've decided to honestly share, and I hope the information will be helpful to you.

Love,
Mom

*W*HY DID GOD GIVE US THE GIFT OF SEX?

Dear Daughters,

An atheist came up to a man and demanded proof that God exists. The answer he received was one word: *sex!* The authors of the book *For Lovers Only* state, "Anybody who has ever experienced great lovemaking instinctively knows the truth: Sex is too good to have just happened. It didn't evolve as the result of some cosmic accident. Something this exquisite had to have been lovingly, brilliantly, creatively designed."[3]

God is the creator of sex, and what an ingenious Creator He is! He lovingly designed man and woman so that their bodies could literally become one. Often I am asked, "Why did God create sex?" Particularly in Eastern Europe and the former Soviet Union where some Christians believe that God created sex only for procreation, this item comes up for discussion.

In the Russian Republic, Christians have told your dad and

me that they believe you can allow yourself pleasure during sex only when you are making a baby! But many wonder, "Why does it feel good if procreation was God's only purpose for creating the sexual relationship?"

Here is what I share with my dear sisters in the East. The Scriptures tell us there are four reasons God created the gift of sex.

1. God gave the gift of sex that we might create life.

Beginning in Genesis, we are commanded to "be fruitful and multiply; fill the earth" (1:28). That may be the only commandment given by God that people have consistently applied. The gift of sex gives us the capability of creating a child from our love. How incredibly creative our God is!

2. God gave the gift of sex for an intimate oneness.

Paul wrote, "For this cause a man shall leave his father and mother, and shall cleave to his wife; and the two shall become one flesh. This mystery is great; but I am speaking with reference to Christ and the church" (Eph. 5:31–32 NASB). God says two can become one flesh. In the most intimate physical act, sexual intercourse, two become one. Have you ever contemplated how miraculous it is that God designed our bodies to literally become one? In the last part of this passage from Ephesians, we're told our "one flesh" is a mystery, but we are to understand that our physical oneness is an earthly picture of the spiritual oneness Christ has with His church.

When I first realized what these verses were *really* saying, I was overwhelmed. How could anyone say God thought sex was wrong or dirty when He, the almighty Creator of the universe, said our oneness physically in marriage is to be a picture of the spiritual oneness He wants to have with us! I think of it this way. It's as if God says to us, "I've given you a visual picture so that when you experience the beauty and intimacy physically, you will have a glimmer, an earthly idea, of all I desire for you spiritually, a oneness of spirit with your Lord." God gave the gift of sex so that we might experience a bonding that encompasses far more than mere physical oneness; it is a joining of body, soul, and spirit.

3. God gave the gift of sex for pleasure.

Procreation and an intimate oneness are two reasons God created sex, but God also created sex for our pleasure. In fact, the Scripture talks much more about the pleasures of sex than it does about "being fruitful" and "being one."

Listen to what God says: "Drink from your own well, my son—be faithful and true to your wife. Let your manhood be a blessing; rejoice in the wife of your youth. Let her charms and tender embrace satisfy you. Let her love alone fill you with delight" (Prov. 5:15, 18–19 TLB). A beautiful parallel is drawn here between thirst being quenched by drinks of cool, fresh water and a couple's sexual thirst being satisfied by exciting, pleasurable sexual union in marriage. My favorite translation of this passage is: "Let your love and your sexual embrace with your wife intoxicate you continually with delight. Always enjoy the ecstasy of her love."

In the Song of Solomon, God devoted an entire book of the Bible to the subject of sexual pleasure in marriage. Your father's book *Solomon on Sex* is a detailed explanation and application of this wonderful little book on married love.

4. God gave the gift of sex for comfort.

If at this point, you're saying, "Really, Mom!" just listen to the Scriptures. In 2 Samuel, we read an account of the death of David and Bathsheba's son, and while grieving, "David comforted Bathsheba his wife, and went in to her and lay with her. So she bore a son, and he called his name Solomon" (12:24).

One woman shared with me that when her husband was in despair over losing his job, loving him physically was a comfort and encouragement to him. Cinda, married to an intense man, said that when her husband had spent his day at the office slaying dragons and experienced little success, she knew she could comfort him and help him relax by loving him physically. Part of the "comfort" God gave was the tension released in lovemaking. A back rub is good for tense bodies, a sexual release even better!

After I shared these four reasons for God's creation of the gift of sex, the women in Russia and Romania who had been skeptical were pleasantly surprised. After all, they wanted to believe that sex was for pleasure as well as for procreation. God was ingenious in His creation. Through our lovemaking we can create life, experience one-flesh intimacy, have pleasure, and even comfort each other in times of stress or sorrow. God's gift is for us to enjoy!

I love you,
Mom

$\mathcal{H}$OW DO YOU PUT IT ALL TOGETHER IN REAL LIFE?

Dear Joy and Robin,

So, my daughters, how do you put making babies, having an intimate oneness, pleasure, and comfort together? Listen to one woman's description of the total oneness she felt after a beautiful time of lovemaking:

I awoke in the middle of the night, everything was dark. I could hear my lover breathing next to me. I snuggled up to him and as my body pressed against his, I felt the warmth again of being close. I lay with my arm around him, reliving the beauty and incredible erotic feelings we had experienced together last night. As we made love in front of the fireplace, it was as if our oneness reached a new height and depth. It's all so tied together. Talking and sharing our deep feelings for an hour before making love gave us such an emotional oneness and that carried over into the physical. I'm sure some Christians would be "shocked" by our free physical abandonment with one another but how pure and right it is! Experiencing the incredible physical ecstasy with one another is like the "frosting on the cake," it binds us close and adds "spice" to our spiritual, emotional, and intellectual oneness. As I feel his warm body now pressed to me,

I laugh inside at how some would not believe two, not so young people, a pastor and his wife no less, could so love sex! The lingering feelings of joy and love, of deep satisfaction and peace, fill me with thankfulness for this man, my husband, and I find myself here in the dark beside him praising God for His gift of oneness, thanking Him for the delights of sexual joy, and asking Him to show me anew how to cherish this man God has given me.

In lovemaking, there is beautiful intimacy, but there should also be laughter, fun, teasing, joy, and variety. God gave sex for pleasure and pleasure is good! It's not wrong or ungodly to simply delight in your spouse's body. Listen to another woman's description of a night of fun and pleasure:

I woke up this morning laughing to myself, no one ever told me sex could be so much fun. It was so hot last night, Dan and I decided to pull our mattress out onto our closed-in veranda. We brought glasses of cool lemonade, and lay on the mattress sipping our drinks, looking at the stars and talking. I felt like a seventh grader at a slumber party! Dan said he was still hot so off came his clothes and of course, then, he decided I'd feel cooler without mine. We buried our faces in our pillows because we were laughing so hard. Making love in the fresh air was a new sensation; I liked it! We kept giggling for fear the neighbors would hear. The sensual feelings were so strong, the slight breeze on our bodies so nice after the hot apartment. I'm glad sex can be such fun and feel so good.

Sadly, some Christian women couldn't enjoy sex on the veranda. They can enjoy the sexual relationship only if they incorporate something spiritual into the physical. For some, it means praying before making love. For one couple, it means singing the doxology together as they climax. (Yes, this is for real.)

Please understand. There is nothing wrong with singing praises to God, being thankful to Him for the gift of sex, or praying before you make love. Praying together before or after loving each other can be very special. I'm just stressing the point that you don't have to "be spiritual" to be granted permission by God to "be physical."

So what I'm trying to say is this: it's okay to tease all day long about what's coming later, to laugh, take a shower together, and slip into bed or on the floor and pleasure, pleasure, pleasure.

It's okay to grab your man after he's been away on a trip and love each other quickly, saying, "More to come tonight after the kids are in bed." It's okay to comfort your man by loving him physically.

Anything is okay as long as you both agree. There is not always an hour of sharing before lovemaking, not always an unlimited amount of time to talk, play, and love. Just as each time we talk with our best friends, it can be different, so each time we love our lovers, it can be unique. How tragic that some love relationships become like this woman's: "Every time it's the same. He touches me for five minutes, always in the same way. I touch him briefly, he enters me, moves in and out, and it's over."

No wonder people think sex is boring! I'd be bored too! Lovemaking can be with laughter; it can be with tears. Incredibly, it can create a child. It can bring oneness or great physical pleasure. It can bring comfort and release tension. Sex is God's gift to His people. Use His gift wisely; use it freely; use it often!

Love,
Mom

$\int$EX IS FOR PLEASURE, BUT HOW MUCH IS OKAY?

Dear Daughters,

What a joy it was to be in Romania, seated around a table with women who were teaching *Partenera Creatora (Creative Counterpart* in Romanian) to small groups of women. After talking to them through a translator on the subject of marriage, I opened it up for questions. Immediately, one dear woman, Lydia, said, "The last paragraph on page 99." It was a statement, not a question, so I asked the translator what Lydia meant. After a long discussion, I was told that this paragraph was disturbing to Lydia because it seemed to imply a great deal of freedom in the sexual relationship, and Lydia was afraid that wasn't spiritual. I knew only one paragraph in *Creative Counterpart* that might be controversial, and it was found on page 196 of the English version. And yes, that was the passage troubling Lydia. It reads, "I believe, from Scripture, that any way you want to touch, kiss, fondle, and love your husband's body or be loved yourself is right and good in God's eyes. The limits are what is pleasurable to both of you."[4]

In 1964 when I married, sexual discussions were held quietly,

usually behind closed doors, and controversial trials were held in private. Mothers did not have to censor news magazines because of lurid sexual details. This year alone, the world has been "treated" to both the Clarence Thomas/Anita Hill hearings and the William Kennedy Smith trial. How lucky can we be? What was once private is blared loudly and not always tastefully.

Times have changed. You and your friends have asked me without much embarrassment about every sexual practice written about so glibly in the news magazines. Whatever you heard about, you asked, and I'm thankful that you came to me.

Now, as you prepare for marriage, I'm sure you're asking, "What are the rules for a married couple who are Christians? Has God established sexual boundaries?" The answer is, "Yes." To set the record straight biblically, here is what the Bible has to say about the kinds of sexual activities prohibited in marriage. As far as I can discern, *what is not prohibited is permitted!* Since I am not a Greek scholar, I asked your dad, who is, to give me a list of the Greek words for these prohibitions along with their true meaning. There are ten prohibitions on the list. I think you will agree with me after reading them that much freedom and variety and pleasure are left for us to enjoy. On to Dad's list:

1. *Fornication.* What is it? It comes from the Greek word *porneia,* which included sleeping with your stepmother (1 Cor. 5:1), sex with a prostitute (1 Cor. 6:13), sexual intercourse outside marriage (1 Cor. 7:2; 1 Thess. 4:3), and adultery (Matt. 5:32).

2. *Adultery.* We all know that this refers to sex with someone to whom you are not married. Scripture has strong words for this sin, even when it is only a mental sin (Matt. 5:28).

3. *Homosexuality*. The Bible is very clear in its opposition to this sexual practice (Lev. 18:22; 20:13; Rom. 1:27; 1 Cor. 6:9).

4. *Impurity and debauchery*. Impurity is often warned against in the New Testament. Several Greek words are translated "impurity." To become "impure" (Greek, *molyno*) can mean to lose one's virginity[5] or to become defiled due to living out a secular and essentially pagan lifestyle (2 Cor. 7:1). The word *rupos* often refers to moral uncleanness in general (Rev. 22:11).

5. *Orgies*. A married couple's involvement in sex orgies with different couples is an obvious violation of (1), (2), and (4), and I don't think it even needs to be discussed.

6. *Prostitution*. Obviously, this is paying for sex. You grew up seeing the ladies of the night in their outlandish costumes on the streets of Vienna, counting them as we drove past. Prostitution is morally wrong according to the Bible.

7. *Lustful passions*. First, let me tell you what this does *not* mean. Lustful passion does not refer to the powerful, God-given sexual desire for each other enjoyed by a married man and woman. Instead, it refers to an unrestrained, indiscriminate sexual desire for men or women other than the person's marriage partner.

8. *Sodomy*. Some Christians have erroneously equated this term with oral sex, but that is not the way the term was used in the Bible. The sodomites in the Bible were male homosexuals[6] or temple prostitutes (both male and female).[7] In the Old Testament, it often refers to men lying with men,[8] but it has nothing to do with the relationship between a husband and wife. The English word means "male homosexual intercourse" or "intercourse with animals."[9]

9. *Obscenity and coarse jokes.* The Scriptures clearly prohibit these things in Ephesians 4:29 where Paul told us that no "unwholesome" word is to come out of our mouths (NASB). The word literally means "rotten" or "decaying." We are also told to avoid "foolish talking" (Eph. 5:4), which in the Greek means "to turn a phrase well." We have all been around people who can see a sexual connotation in some innocent phrase and then begin to snicker or laugh about it, which is "coarse jesting." That would rule out not sexual humor in marriage but the public and inappropriate jokes heard in the locker room.

10. *Incest.* Incest is specifically forbidden in Scripture (Lev. 18:7–18; 20:11–21). Nothing more need be said.

So, my daughters, you have the ten things forbidden within marriage, the rules for a married couple who are Christians. As you can see, there is *lots* of room for what you can do within the marriage bond. As I said before, "If it is not prohibited, it is permitted."

One wise man stated, "You may do anything you wish so long as it harms neither of you and involves no one else." Good wisdom. There is great freedom in our use of God's gift of sex so I repeat what so disturbed Lydia:

- I believe, from Scripture, that any way you want to touch, kiss, fondle, and love your husband's body or be loved yourself is right and good in God's eyes. The limits are what is pleasurable to both of you.

- If it is not prohibited, it is permitted.

- You may do anything you wish so long as it harms neither of you and involves no one else.

The above three statements are wise advice from your mom, your dad, and a wise counselor. Together with your husband, you can discover the "limits" for you. The freedom is great, the beauty of discovery exciting. Have fun discovering each other!

Much love,
Mom

$\mathcal{W}$HAT IS CREATIVE SEX COMMUNICATION?

Dear Daughters,

I hope you are ready for this! There actually was a book written that gave this sterling advice about sex communication: "The only time husband and wife can 'licitly' discuss their 'conjugal relations' is when it is necessary to the successful completion of the act." (I guess that's when they don't know when and where to put what!) Obviously, the author was of the anything-fun-must-be-a-sin camp!

In the Song of Solomon the lovers share openly, honestly, deliberately but delicately, describing each other physically, complimenting each others sexual charms, and explicitly detailing what pleases them sexually. (I told you the Bible was the best book on sex!)

Communication in every facet of marriage is vital but especially in the most intimate area, the arena of lovemaking. One

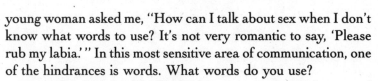

young woman asked me, "How can I talk about sex when I don't know what words to use? It's not very romantic to say, 'Please rub my labia.'" In this most sensitive area of communication, one of the hindrances is words. What words do you use?

One school of thought holds that since our sexual acts and sexual parts have scientifically correct names, we can solve sexual communication problems easily by using these "right words." As one wise woman put it, "This might be all right if we are going to talk about sex only in a scientific way (fine for Masters and Johnson and my gynecologist) but terribly dull in the bedroom. Those words make sex sound so depressingly clinical. I don't want to engage in precoital stimulation. I want to play sex games with my man."

Words are a problem. One could, of course, rely on sensual Braille, which could be fun but sometimes also leads to misinterpretations. We want to clearly and specifically communicate with our lovers because we long for that intimate oneness and pleasure that God created us to enjoy, and God has a very creative solution!

The medical terms leave a feeling of mechanics, and the slang terms raise a psychological censor in some, so the Lord avoided both problems in the Bible by using poetic symbolism. Now if this sounds too far out, listen to Solomon's bride describing him physically:

> My beloved is dazzling and
>   ruddy,
> Outstanding among ten
>   thousand.

His head is like gold, pure gold;
His locks are like clusters of
    dates,
And black as a raven.
His eyes are like doves,
Beside streams of water,
Bathed in milk,
And reposed in their setting.
His cheeks are like a bed of
    balsam,
Banks of sweet-scented herbs;
His lips are lilies,
Dripping with liquid myrrh.
His hands are rods of gold
Set with beryl;
His abdomen is carved ivory
Inlaid with sapphires.
His legs are pillars of alabaster
Set on pedestals of pure gold;
His appearance is like Lebanon,
Choice as the cedars.
His mouth is full of sweetness.
And he is wholly desirable.
This is my beloved and this is my
    friend. (Song 5:10–16 NASB)

To me, this is one of the most beautiful descriptions. As I told you, I especially love the ending: "This is my beloved and this is my friend. He is wholly desirable." Solomon and his bride used special poetic words to communicate delicately when it was hard to find the right word. Three guesses what "garden" means in these passages:

> Make my garden breathe out fragrance,
> Let its spices be wafted abroad.
> May my beloved come into his garden
> And eat its choice fruits!
> I have come into my garden, my sister, my bride;
> I have gathered my myrhh along with my balsam.
> I have eaten my honeycomb and my honey;
> I have drunk my wine and my milk
>   (Song 4:16—5:1 NASB).

In a delicate and erotic way, "garden" refers to the bride's genitals, and in another passage in the Song of Solomon, "fruit" refers to the groom's. God's solution was to use poetry. But what if you feel as silly using poetic terms as you do mechanical, medical terms? Then make up your own names!

One man suggested the following:

Some weekend afternoon before you make love, take the time to assign innocent names to all of each other's "crucial" body parts. You get to invent the names for your husband's, and he has the privilege of naming yours. As he lies back in bed against his pillow, fondly look him over and give each part a kiss as you name it: "I dub thee Larry; I dub thee Norman and thee Nicholas; I dub thee Sir William the Great." Then, it's your turn to arrange yourself just so and allow your husband to enjoy a long, loving look. Let him plant an affectionate kiss on each of your feminine charms as he names them: "I title thee Louella; I title thee Tammy and thee Claretta and thee Lady Katherine."[10]

You can make up any names you want. Invent private, special names that only you and your beloved know. These secret names will help you communicate; somehow it is just less awkward to say, "Baby, Claretta really needs you tonight," instead of "I want you to come into my vagina tonight."

Private names make it possible to communicate in other ways. How about a card sent to your lover signed, "All my love, Claretta." Or a telephone call to your husband, asking if he's been in touch with Claretta, telling him it is urgent that they make contact before the next day. There are all sorts of possibilities. Obviously, your private names must be strictly private, and it would probably be good if you didn't know people by the same names.

Learning to communicate about your sexual needs and desires takes time, but it is worth the time and even fun! Choose to swallow embarrassment, choose to open up the secret places of your heart, mind, and body to your beloved, and he will truly grow to become your beloved and your friend!

I love you both,
Mom

CAN MY HUSBAND REALLY SENSE MY SEXUAL ATTITUDE?

Dear Daughters,

When I wrote *Creative Counterpart* in 1977, few Christian women were talking about the sexual relationship in marriage. Your father had written *Solomon on Sex* the same year, and with two books dealing with sexual issues, I felt I was labeled as one who speaks and writes about "those things." At one point I told your father that I thought I would hide in the house for several weeks so people wouldn't stare at me. I was sure they were whispering together and saying, "I bet she even *does* those things she and her husband wrote about!" This is just one of the joys of being an author.

I felt it was important to talk about the physical aspect of marriage in 1977, and I feel it even more strongly now. At the end of the chapters on sex in *Creative Counterpart,* I talk about the importance of a wife being available to her husband, aggressive toward him sexually, and creative in their lovemaking. I end with this statement:

> There are many creative things I can suggest, but you must start thinking and come up with your own. Remember, special times together are important and cannot be stressed enough, but the most important thing is your ATTITUDE.

Does your husband know you are available and excited about him as your lover? God gave him to you as your beloved and your friend. Let him in on the secret![11]

What attitude does your husband receive from you about your love life? I remember a friend stating it like this: "When he walks out of the shower, what attitude does he sense from you? Do you walk up to him and put your arms around his slightly wet body, kiss him, and tell him how good he looks to you? Or do you run the other way in fear that if your attitude is positive, he will get 'ideas'? Does your attitude say, 'I am excited about you and moving toward you,' or 'I am not excited about you and am moving away from you'?"

Remember, an attitude is an inward feeling expressed by behavior and can be seen without a word being said. Attitudes are expressed by our body language and by the looks on our faces. What are we expressing to our lovers and best friends?

I can just hear you saying, "But, Mom, is a wife *always* supposed to have a positive attitude about sex? What about when she is tired, depressed, or hurried, or she just plain isn't in the mood?"

In my letters to you about communication, I stressed the importance of honest, open sharing. This is true in every part of your relationship, including the sexual. The question is: How are your honesty and openness expressed? What *attitude* is communicated to this man you love?

- "I'm too busy for you. Can't you see I have other things on my mind? Is sex all you ever think about?"

- "Honey, I'm whipped. The day has been awful. I don't think there is any way my body can respond to anything but a hot bath and sleep. But I would love to love you. . . . Let me make you feel good. Tomorrow will be another day, and I'll be ready for you to pleasure me and be a full partner in our lovemaking."

Both statements are honest, but one is selfish and one is loving; one presents a negative attitude, the other a positive. Whether we are aware of it or not, an attitude is being projected; our men *sense* either our love or our rejection.

I must clarify. In the letters I wrote about sex, I said that the wife should be a full partner in the lovemaking, be totally involved and responsive, and that it was just as important for her to be satisfied as it was for her husband. What I have just said in this letter does not negate that. Both are true. The norm is that both are always involved; the exception is that one can satisfy the other in a loving and caring way.

Let me share with you the story of one woman. I will call her Jenna. I came to greatly respect Jenna as I grieved with her, wept with her, and watched her choose a beautiful attitude that so honored God.

Jenna had no sexual feelings. She was married to a wonderful and loving Christian man. She was terrified that because of her inability to respond, he would tire of making love to a "board" who just lay there unresponsively (that was her description) and turn to another woman.

Jenna knew why her sexual feelings were locked up. When she was twelve, her older sister had become pregnant. The distraught mother held Jenna across her lap and begged Jenna to promise her that she would never do anything like her sister had done. Jenna promised, and when she began to date and had sexual feelings, she rejected them. From her perspective, sex was something that brought pain and an unwanted baby. Besides, she had promised her mother.

Years of rejecting her God-given sexual feelings resulted in them being so deeply buried that she couldn't find them when both she and her husband desperately longed for her response.

Thus far, professionals had not been able to help, so Jenna had come to me. After sharing all I knew from Scripture, praying, suggesting, I said, "Jenna, I don't know what God will do. I know He can release you, but I can't promise you He will. I can only tell you what my choice would be if I were in your place. If today I knew that I would never have another sexual feeling, would never experience again the joy of sharing heights of pleasure with my man, with God's help, this would be my attitude.

To choose to become an incredible, fantastic, and creative lover to my man. To seek to know and understand his needs, his dreams, his desires, and to meet them. To become all he had ever longed for in a lover. To emotionally enter into lovemaking with every fiber of my being, and to trust God for the physical feelings. If the feelings did not come, I would be at peace that I was loving my man with all I had to give.

As I shared this with Jenna, I told her that I knew what I was saying was difficult, very difficult. Several months later, she said,

"I still don't have feelings, but I am more at peace. You're right. I don't have to be a board, and giving so much emotionally and physically to my husband has given much to me. Attitude does play a big part. I just pray I can continue to have this positive attitude and trust God for the feelings. My husband sure likes the 'new me.'"

Well, my daughters, my observations tell me that you are not lacking in sexual feelings. (That's why I've spent the last years on my knees!) But you will have choices to make because you will be tired, there will be times when you want to crawl into bed alone, so how will you be honest and still love your man?

You can suggest that you wait until another time when you are more alert, you can say you want to love *him* but don't feel like you can respond, or you can say, "Lord, You know how I feel, blah. But I love this man, and I want to show him my love even though I don't feel like it right this minute. Teach me to love him. I choose to love him now."

Attitude isn't everything, but it is a lot. It's been said that a woman's sexiest organ is her brain. When I choose to dwell on loving my man, regardless of my feelings, amazing things happen. Some of our most beautiful times together have been when "I wasn't in the mood."

I love you,
Mom

CREATIVE GIFT GIVING

Dear Daughers,

A wise woman once observed, "You can become a Rembrandt in your sexual art, or you can stay at the paint-by-numbers stage." The woman who would never think of serving her husband the same microwave dinner every night sometimes serves him the same sexual response time after time after time. Sex, like supper, loses much of its flavor when it becomes totally predictable.

A very famous author (your father) says, "It is *biblical* for a wife to be a skillful and creative lover to her husband."[12] Solomon said of his bride's love skill:

> How beautiful is your love, my sister, my bride!
> How much better is your love than wine.
> (Song 4:10 NASB).

To be creative is to bring into existence something that hasn't been there before. When applied to the sexual relationship, it means to bring into existence a vital and invigorating perspective. A man I know, Pat, wins the prize for bringing into existence a beach in the dead of winter! How could a beach be fun without the sun to tan you and the water to entice you?

Pat's wife had left him alone one weekend with the children

while she traveled to another state to be the matron of honor in a dear friend's wedding. He missed her mothering skills and her cooking expertise, but most of all he missed her loving. To welcome her home, he created a beach in a spare room, put the children to bed early, and waited patiently for his lover to return.

What a special surprise awaited this lucky wife. The weather was cold and dreary, but inside it was summer! Her loving man had carted numerous bags of sand to create his beach. Candles, beach towels, music of flowing water, a special picnic lunch—all added to the beach effect! A creative way to say, "I love you. I love loving you."

When the evening was over, of course, Pat and his wife had several bags of used sand to dispose of. What did they do? Easy! They put them in a big wooden box in the backyard, and voilá, a sandbox for the kids! Now that is what I call creative recycling.

One woman asked, "What if the creative stuff isn't as fulfilling as the old standby ways of making love?" No ifs about it. Sand sticks to your body, particularly if you have given each other a back or body rub with lotion! When you try the floor instead of the bed, you may end up the next day with a sore back or carpet burns! If you sneak out in the middle of the night to enjoy your love by the light of the silvery moon, you may find that mosquitoes have eaten you alive. But that is not the point. You were adventurers, and you've made a special memory, even if it turned out to be a hilarious disaster! You've stirred up the water of your marriage to keep it from going *stagnant*. So now that you're convinced that creativity is good, consider these ideas.

One clever wife who had no money available to buy her husband a birthday gift created his favorite present of all time with only three-by-five cards, felt-tip markers, and yarn. (Not too big an investment!) What possible gift could a wife make with these meager supplies? A coupon book, filled with coupons redeemable whenever her husband wished. The type of coupon made this simple paper gift such a success:

1. Back rub with hot oil.
2. Bubble bath for two by candlelight.
3. Picnic in the raw (can be inside where it's safe or outside if you're brave).
4. I'm your slave for a day.
5. I make love to you; you be my guide.
6. You make love to me; I'll be your guide.
7. Breakfast in bed . . . with me.

I'm sure you can now see why the coupon book was a hit! Lack of money seems to bring out creativity in all of us. Two young married lovers had low funds and decided that instead of buying each other Christmas gifts, they would pool their available resources and give themselves a night at a fancy hotel in town. With picnic basket in hand, candles, a tape recorder, and tapes of soft music, they were ready for a Christmas gift to remember. I am certain the memories from the gift will linger much longer than a new sweater.

Writing to you about creative gifts brings to my mind the most creative of all, given to me by your father. The remembrance is a poignant one because it is also a reminder of my biggest failure.

Let me set the scene for you. It was 1971. I had three children, and the oldest was three. I was tired, exhausted, numb. The thing I remember most about that year is the doctor's office; I was there almost every week because you children were continually sick. I felt there was no end to what needed to be done—I was a robot, trying to do it all.

Because of my tiredness, my sexual desire was at a very low ebb so I wrote T.S. (T.S. = Think Sex) on my calendar every couple of days to remind me to think about sex. Yes, I was trying but still failed miserably when your father used every creative bone in his body and gave me a "capsule gift." What was it? A prescription bottle of fifty-two pills in capsule form, each empty capsule filled not with medication but with a creative surprise for each week of the year. The label on the bottle read: "For Linda Dillow, prescribed by Dr. Joseph Dillow to alleviate stress. Take one each week." The gift took time to make:

- A trip to a drugstore to get fifty-two capsules. (I can just hear the druggist: "What do you want them for?")
- Much time and thought and creativity to think up and type fifty-two clever ideas.
- Much more time and dexterity to cut fifty-two clever ideas into strips and roll them to fit in the capsules!

No wonder he was hurt when I would forget to take my pill, when my excitement about his special gift was at the same level as my sexual desire. Obviously, our marriage and love life survived my failure, but I wanted to share it with you so you would know that *no* relationship is always perfect. Marriage partners are always two very human people who make many mistakes but keep loving each other, keep forgiving each other, and keep striving to be creative in all areas of their relationship. Creativity in your love life adds zest to what can become commonplace. It's really not the sandbags, the coupons, or the capsules that are as important as the attitude that says, "Honey, our love life together means so much to me that I want to do everything I can to make it exciting."

Love,
Mom

*M*AKING LOVEMAKING A PRIORITY

Dear Daughters,

I was really shocked last year to realize that things I had learned long ago had to be relearned. Very discouraging! Even after so many years of marriage, making my lover relationship with my husband a priority did not come naturally. I thought that with all four of you kids away at college, we would have hours available to be alone. It would be just the two of us, like in the beginning.

It was quiet and the hours were there, but being alone, totally alone, gave me the illusion that there would always be time for lovemaking. Again I had to learn:

- We must *take* the time available.
- We must *make* the time if there is no time.
- We must *plan* the time.

While you are newlyweds, this won't be much of a problem, I'm sure, but before you know it, you will be young marrieds with toddlers and tired! During every stage of married life and even during the empty nest, you will have to choose to love, to make your lover relationship a priority.

You will have to choose intimacy and an exciting sexual relationship because our society places lovemaking at the bottom of the priority list. You will never find the time. You must *make* it. Isn't it amazing how often that little word *choice* creeps in? A wise woman is one whose choice is loving her man!

I have a very creative friend, Anna, who adds fun and excitement to her sexual relationship by making appointments with her husband. Definition of an *appointment:* "a special time set aside to love each other and have a long drawn-out 'intimate oneness' lovemaking session." Perhaps Anna and Nick will schedule an appointment for Friday night or Wednesday lunch or December 10 at 6:30 A.M. For days they will remind each other of their engagement. The reminders are in private but also in public. Both Anna and Nick work in the same office, and Anna has been known to say to Nick as she leaves work: "Don't forget our important meeting Wednesday at noon!" On the morning of the appointment, Anna presses her body close to Nick's, kisses him, and whispers in his ear that she is looking *so* forward to their rendezvous at noon! By lunchtime they are excited and very anxious for their appointment.

Anna said that they don't schedule sex times often, but when they do, they feel like young newlyweds. Oh . . . I forgot to mention that Anna and Nick are in their sixties! Who says sex is only for the young and beautiful firm-bodied bunch?

I recently read statistics reporting that people in their sixties have sexual relations twice a month. They must not have interviewed Anna and Nick!

God's beauty and freedom in sex are available to every married couple. Why do so many miss out on God's best? One reason is that they do not choose to make time to spend with their lovers, to make loving each other a priority.

A second reason is that some young couples have bought into the media lie. As I said previously, the movies project a dramatic and ever-exciting sexual relationship. (They ought to; each sex scene probably had twenty-two retakes!) In comparison, normal everyday people feel clumsy and awkward, without the romance the movies portray. Real people just don't talk like characters in romance novels. Neither do most real people communicate like Solomon and his bride: "My beloved is dazzling and ruddy, Outstanding among ten thousand."

Christian psychologists encourage young couples to learn God's viewpoint of the sexual relationship and not that of the motion pictures:

> Keep in mind that good sex, like good golf, takes practice. Also remember that the media are not training sources; they are fantasy machines. They project a larger-than-life view of sex in order to promote the fantasy. They want to leave you breathless and wide-eyed, not better informed. The cops and robbers don't shoot real bullets in those movies, either. It's an elaborately staged set-up. Your love life is the real thing and, pursued with elan, will provide infinitely

better pleasure and intimacy than any manufactured fantasy.[13]

I encourage you to read what your mom wrote in *Creative Counterpart* about overcoming inhibitions (pages 187–91). Even in this age when nothing sexual is secret, some women are still fearful or embarrassed to let go and be a sexual being. It all starts in the mind, which, in case you didn't know, is a very sexy organ. One man said, "The first organ a person must use to achieve sexual satisfaction is the brain." So how do you renew your mind?

1. Memorize and meditate on God's viewpoint. God says that His Word is like a two-edged sword, piercing into our lives. For whatever reason, wrong priorities, wrong programming, wrong information, many wives need to have their minds reprogrammed. There is no simple method. Memorizing takes work, but placing Proverbs 5:18–19 or the Song of Solomon 5:10–16 in the forefront of your mind makes a difference!

2. Make a choice to be the lover that your husband needs and that God wants you to be. Again, so much of life starts with your choices. Remember that loving lasts a lifetime and is worth the time and effort! My prayer is that in forty years each of you will be like Anna, scheduling appointments with your husband!

Love,
Mom

$\mathcal{W}$HY KEEP THE HOME FIRES BURNING?

Dear Daughters,

The scene was set. We'll call the couple Jack and Jane. Outwardly a good marriage, secretly a silent separation and sex once every few months.

The scenario was simple and sad. One lovely divorcée taking advantage of Jack's moment of weakness. The story is doubly sad because Jack was a missionary, one who wanted to serve God and had sacrificed greatly to go overseas. Jack is now divorced, leaving Jane and three children who don't understand. As he talked, we heard many examples of how he had "fled" when approached in his secular business by women. One woman came into his office and blatantly lifted her dress above her waist and just stood there smiling! (I call that blatant!) It seems that one of the freedoms some women think they have acquired is the freedom to be *very* aggressive toward men.

I can remember saying to friends when Jack left Jane, "You know, we are fortunate. Our husbands travel in Eastern Europe and Russia where women are more old-fashioned and not so aggressive sexually."

Three days after I made that statement, my dear husband brought home a poem he had received from the translator he had used on his last trip to the Ukraine:

Since the night I met you first
There is no one on the Earth
Whom I gave so much a thought
But you and God, yes, you and God.
Then your eyes were shining bright
You spoke of God and you were right
There is one way left for me
To repent and come to Him
But so difficult it is
To retell of all my sins
Before audience so wide
That's what makes my tongue so tied.
I am now at great a loss
What I am and which I was—
Sinful woman? Sinless creature?
Where to find a trustful preacher?
Be it you! Perhaps you could
Lead me out of the wood
Of my sins and of my doubts
And to show my whereabouts.

An English professor, age forty (that may sound old to you, but it is ten years younger than I am!), had poured out her heart to this man, *my* man, who was perhaps the "trustful preacher" who would lead her to the truth.

She poured out her heart. I poured over the poem: "What did she mean, 'bright eyes'? (I studied my husband's eyes.) What did she mean, 'all she'd thought about was him and God'? (If she meant it only in a spiritual sense, why did she talk about his

eyes!)" How pleased God would be if I studied His Word the way I dissected that poem!

Yes, there are lots of women, even in the Ukraine, who would do *anything* to capture my husband and yours. Men who love the Lord, men with character, are *very* attractive to women. A caring, honest, honorable man is a rarity and very appealing to women who have known only the coarse, uncaring variety.

I truly believe that Jack wanted to resist temptation. I also believe he would have been able to if he and Jane had developed an exciting sexual relationship. You notice that I used the word *developed*. The beautiful, free, erotic, all-encompassing relationship God desires for you and your husband takes time—so be patient *and* enjoy the process!

Last year your father gave me a great compliment when he said, "I've never been tempted by another woman." At first I wasn't sure he was serious, but he assured me he was. "Why would I want someone else when I have you waiting for me at home?" was his reply.

Am I beautiful? No. Do I have a gorgeous figure? No. (Cottage cheese on the legs.) Am I at my perfect weight? No. (Always working on it.) *But* do I love my man. Yes! And have I worked for twenty-nine years to learn to be a creative lover? Yes! Has it been worth it? Yes! I pray, my daughters, that you will receive the same compliment when you're an old married lady like me.

Love,
Mom

P.S. Do you think your father has bright eyes?
P.P.S. Next time your dad travels to Kiev, I'm going with him! I'll be the "trustful preacher" who leads her to the truth!

$\mathcal{M}$ARRIAGE: A GIFT EXCHANGE

Dear Daughters,

What gift will you give your husband on your wedding day? I'm not talking about a camera, leather jacket, or watch, but the priceless gift you will present to him after the vows are said and the guests are gone.

It is the gift of your body. Really it is a gift exchange because your new husband also gives his body to you. According to the Scriptures, you actually have ownership of each other physically: "The wife does not have authority over her own body, but the husband does. And likewise the husband does not have authority over his own body, but the wife does" (1 Cor. 7:4).

What an indescribable privilege to be given the body of your husband as a gift! God gave the gift of sex; you exchange the gift of your body with your lover that you might fully enjoy His gift. It's a privilege but also a responsibility.

We, in America, have been granted everything necessary to fully develop the talent of loving our men:

1. *Privacy*. We have a place to call our own where what is done in private is private.
2. *Time*. Even with busy schedules, we have more time available to us than most of the world.

3. *Birth control.* This is readily available so the fear of pregnancy has become a nonissue.
4. *Information.* Books, video series, tapes, and counselors are available if we want them.

A dear Romanian friend, Marianna, had none of these things available to her, yet her desire to be the lover her man desired was strong. She taught me much about hard choices and creativity.

Visiting Marianna in the prerevolution days in Romania, I was astounded at how tiny her apartment was: one *very* small bedroom for five people. The three children slept in the bedroom, Marianna and her husband in the living room.

Privacy was a fantasy seen only in movies. Since Marianna worked five and a half days a week (not because she wanted to but because the system said she had to) and stood in line for food hours each day, tiredness was an ever-present reality. Birth control was nonexistent in Romania, having been forbidden by the dictator, Ceausescu. Information about marriage and the sexual relationship was unheard of, except for a few typed copies of my book *Creative Counterpart,* which circulated around the country.

Marianna had such a copy and had literally memorized it. She told me that this was her prayer to God: "Dear Lord, it seems impossible that we can have an exciting sexual relationship, but I want this and I ask You to show me how to be creative in my circumstances."

How God must rejoice over a heart like Marianna's! And God did show her. I sat in her small living room as she shared with a group of Romanian women how her love relationship with her husband had grown. She related how she had decided to rest for one-half hour after work so she would have the energy to stay up later than her eighteen-year-old son; how she had saved for months and taken her husband to a hotel for a night; how she and her husband often took walks around their ugly block apartment so they could talk and share in private.

As Marianna talked, I sank into my chair, convicted. How much she did with so little. This verse came to my mind: "To whom much is given . . . much will be required" (Luke 12:48). How very much I had been given. Being a creative lover was easy for me, maybe too easy.

You must ask yourself, What am I doing with the "much" I have been given? You have authority over your husband's body. How do you use that ownership? You have privacy and time to develop God's gift. Surely with all you have, God does require more of you in your choices and creativity.

The statistics reveal that the number one need for a husband in the marriage relationship is sexual fulfillment.[14] Are your choices taking you in the direction of meeting his need? Are your choices taking you toward an exciting, intimate oneness where you truly become his beloved and he becomes yours?

As you give your priceless gift to your new husband, give it with this prayer of commitment: "I give you my body, that with it I might bring you ecstasy. I choose to continually grow to be creative, available, aggressive, to be all you could ever desire in a lover. I pray that together we might choose to continually grow to learn more about God's gift of sex, that we might more each year experience the intimate oneness and pleasure of His wonderful gift!"

Love,
Mom

6
GIVING VS. GETTING

ℒOOKING FOR THE STARS?

Dear Daughters,

There is really very little difference in people, but that little difference makes a big difference because the little difference is attitude. The big difference is whether it is positive or negative, and that depends on what we choose. The following story about a young bride graphically illustrates this.

In the fairy tales, the bride and groom ride away on a white horse and live happily ever after. In real life, the groom had to go to war, and the bride had to choose to live without her beloved or follow him to an army camp on the edge of the desert in California. Being an East Coast girl, the young bride had to make quite an adjustment.

Living conditions were primitive at best. Her husband suggested that she not move, but she desperately wanted to be with him. The heat was unbearable, 115 degrees in the shade, and the wind blew constantly, sending dust and sand everywhere. The only house they could find was a run-down shack near an Indian village, and to top it off, her Indian neighbors spoke very little English. With dirt, dust, constant heat, and no one to talk to, the days became long and boring for the young bride. When her husband was ordered farther into the desert for two weeks of maneuvers, loneliness and the horrible living conditions con-

vinced her that she couldn't take anymore, and she wrote her
mother that she was coming home.

Her very astute mother replied quickly with a letter that included just two lines:

> Two men looked through prison bars,
> One saw mud, the other saw stars.

The young bride read the two lines over and over until she saw
the attitude she had created. Her situation *was* awful, but she had
chosen to dwell only on the awfulness and had not tried to see
anything positive. She did want to be with her husband, so she
determined to look for the stars.

In the following days, she set out to make friends with the
Indians, asking them to teach her weaving and pottery making.
At first they were distant, but as soon as they sensed her genuine
interest, they returned her friendship. She became interested in
their culture and history, and as she began to study the desert, it
changed from a desolate, forbidding place to a marvelous thing
of beauty. And would you believe that the young bride became
such an expert on the forms of the cacti, the yuccas, the Joshua
trees, on everything in the desert, that eventually she wrote a
book about it?

What had changed? Not the desert; not the Indians. The
young bride created her own "happily ever after" by changing
her own attitude and, in the process, making one groom very
happy indeed.[1]

I like this story better than fairy tales because it's real life

where love is forged out of difficult circumstances, where real people grow and become better people and thus have much more love to give.

Lots to think about, isn't there? Important things to think about. I really like the mother's two-sentence reply to her daughter's letter. Let's determine together to look for the stars! Our attitude touches every area of our love relationship.

I love you,
Mom

$\mathscr{T}$HE 100/100 PLAN

Dear Daughters,

It is 6:00 A.M., and I am tired! After being up all night long, I can testify that jet lag is a real thing! Being Gypsies for Jesus has its advantages; it is exciting to travel around the world, but although my *spirit* is willing, my *body* is rebelling at this Gypsy existence.

When I spend the night awake, it is a good time to think and pray. Last night my thoughts were of a conversation I had yesterday with a young woman named Chris. The conversation went like this:

CHRIS: "Jim just doesn't meet my needs. He's not sensitive to me."

ME: "Why don't you make a reservation for dinner for two and take Jim out tonight so you can talk alone together?"

CHRIS: "No, it's up to him to make a reservation. He knows I like to go out to dinner."

ME: "Chris, recently I asked Jody to share with me how I could better meet his needs. Why don't you ask Jim tonight how you can better love him?"

CHRIS: "I know what he'd say—sex, sex, sex—and I try hard enough. He needs to change, not me. I can't do my 50 percent in this marriage if he isn't doing his 50 percent."

Chris talked about a 50/50 plan of marriage that says, "You do your part, and I'll do mine." The concept sounds logical, but couples who try it are destined for disappointment. As one man observed, "The husband or wife who says 'I'll meet you halfway, dear,' is usually a poor judge of distance."

The 50/50 plan will fail because it is impossible to determine if your mate has met you halfway. When neither partner can agree where *halfway* is, each is left to scrutinize the other's performance from a selfish perspective.[2]

Thomas Fuller remarked, "Each horse thinks his pack is the heaviest." How true of marriage! Often both husband and wife are busy, overworked, tired, and feel taken for granted. The real question isn't who put in the hardest day's work or who had the most pressures and hassles. The real question is, How do you build oneness instead of waiting for the other person to meet you halfway?[3] How do you concentrate on *give* instead of *get* in the relationship?

Marriage will never work with the 50/50 plan, a tit-for-tat relationship where you keep score. Sometimes I think the world is

full of people all waiting for someone to meet *their* needs. It's a more grown-up version of the "I won't play dolls with you unless you play house with me" routine. "You be nice to me; I'll be nice to you"—balancing the scales to make sure we get as much as we give. Marriage will never work with this attitude.

God's plan for marriage is a 100/100 plan based on how Jesus lived His life. Why did Christ come to earth? The gospel of Mark proclaims, "For even the Son of Man did not come to be served, but to serve, and to give His life a ransom for many" (10:45).

Christ came to serve, to give, and to sacrifice. What do I mean by *serve?* In our world today, serving is often taken to mean doing menial tasks or waiting on someone. In a recent university psychology class these statistics were given concerning what the average housewife does during her lifetime:

- Cooks 35,000 meals

- Makes from 10,000–40,000 beds

- Vacuums a rug a mile long and a tenth of a mile wide

- Cleans 7,000 plumbing fixtures[4]

Wives do *many* tasks that are not what I would call pleasant. I laughed at the term *plumbing fixtures;* such a delicate way to say, "Clean the toilet." Wives have unpleasant tasks, but husbands do too. All people have things written into their job descriptions they would prefer not to do; that is just part of life but *not* what Christ meant by *serving.*

God's 100/100 plan for marriage states, I choose to do everything I can to love you, without demanding an equal amount in return.

That is what it means to serve, to minister, to give. How very difficult it is because it goes against every self-centered bone in our bodies! First, we have to realize that our selfishness is wrong, and then see what we can do about it!

Much love,
Mom

𝒯HE GREATEST THREAT TO ONENESS

Dear Daughters,

I
ME
MINE
MYSELF

The four words stood out in bold print, appearing to form an enormous monument. At the base of the strange edifice were hundreds of people with arms uplifted, as if worshiping at an altar. And then in very small letters, this caption appeared at the bottom of the editorial cartoon: "Speaking of American cults . . ."

Surrounding the borders of the cartoon were four very familiar lines from well-known commercials:

Have it your way.
Do yourself a favor.
You owe it to yourself.
You deserve a break today.[5]

Where does our selfishness come from? We are fed it daily in subtle ways; it is the "cult" of our era. Christopher Lasch wrote *The Culture of Narcissism,*[5] a book that the *New York Daily News* called "a biting new study of present day society." Lasch says about today's advertising: "It serves not so much to advertise products as to promote consumption as a way of life. The modern propaganda of commodities and the good life has sanctioned impulse gratification."

Lasch's book became a national best-seller because it struck a chord with readers who instinctively knew he was right. Our narcissistic society continually feeds our ravenous appetite for self-satisfaction. Indulgent toward our own needs and indifferent toward the needs of others (particularly marriage partners), we have become in part a society that knows little of true self-sacrifice and self-denial. Dennis Rainey asserts, "Selfishness is possibly the most dangerous threat to oneness that any marriage can face." It keeps us from being faithful to do our 100 percent: to choose to do everything to love our men without demanding an equal amount in return.

How very far we have fallen from the commandment of Jesus: "Let nothing be done through selfish ambition or conceit, but in lowliness of mind let each esteem others better than himself. Let each of you look out not only for his own interests, but also for the interests of others" (Phil. 2:3–4).

Often as Christians, we apply these verses to *others;* it is easier to accept and forgive someone we don't live with day in, day out, every day, and forever. It is easy to get our thinking wrong and buy into the "I, Me, Mine, Myself" mentality. Sacrifice is the only answer to selfishness. Jesus came to minister, not to be min-

istered to. Am I saying it is easy? Not for a moment. It is incredibly difficult for me, for you; just like it was for Christ.

Listen, my daughters, to these beautiful words of the apostle Paul from 1 Corinthians 13. They are familiar words, so it is easy to not really *hear* what love is. Listen carefully to them:

Love is very patient and kind, never jealous or envious, never boastful or proud, never haughty or selfish or rude. Love does not demand its own way. It is not irritable or touchy. It does not hold grudges and will hardly even notice when others do it wrong. It is never glad about injustice, but rejoices whenever truth wins out. If you love someone you will be loyal to him no matter what the cost. You will always believe in him, always expect the best of him, and always stand your ground in defending him. (vv. 4–7 TLB)

I remember during our first year of marriage, being challenged by a friend to read 1 Corinthians 13 out loud, putting my name where it said *love*. I got halfway through the passage, and it was hard to continue because the words sounded so untrue: "Linda is very patient and kind, Linda is not selfish or rude, irritable or touchy. Linda does not demand her own way." A stark contrast from the monument of **I, ME, MINE, MYSELF**. Love erases the selfishness and replaces it with sacrificing self for the beloved. Sacrifice is the answer to selfishness.

Love is giving, not getting.
Love is caring, not controlling.
Love is sacrifice, not selfishness.

Love is making hard choices to give, to care, to sacrifice even when it hurts, even when no ones sees but God.

Obviously, since God's plan for marriage is 100/100, both partners are to strive to give, to choose to do their part to love. I pray your husbands will strive to be 100 percent men, but what will your choice be if they don't?

We *must* choose to be faithful, not because of what we will get or because the others are being faithful, but because God has asked us to be faithful. Again, I repeat, we can be responsible only for what we can control, for our 100 percent. But help! How can we do this? It seems impossible. There are no easy answers, but I'll share some thoughts with you in my next letter.

I love you,
Mom

$\mathcal{F}$OLLOWING THE SERVANT KING

Dear Daughters,

Who was Jesus Christ? A leader? Definitely a leader. But what kind of leader? Authoritarian? No. Unique among men, unique among leaders, He exemplified a radical new form of leadership, the servant leader.

How was it possible? The King said, "I came not to be ministered unto but to minister, the first shall be last and the last first." A servant leader. Our great King and Lord is a servant who

made the ultimate sacrifice in giving His life a ransom for many. And we are to be like Him.

Therefore, a teacher is to be a servant teacher, a businessperson a servant businessperson, a lawyer a servant lawyer, a builder a servant builder, and a wife a servant wife.

How the modern feminists rail against such an idea . . . but Jesus did it first. To Him, it was a privilege to give, to serve, to sacrifice. I've thought much about this. If Jesus gave His life, can I do less? Can I not sacrifice for those I love?

Being a wife is a sacrificial role. Whenever we love unconditionally, it is a sacrifice of self. Whenever we care about another's hurts, successes, and failures more than our own, it is a sacrifice of self. Whenever we compromise, it is a sacrifice of self. It hurts to sacrifice; it's hard to sacrifice; it's a daily learning process to sacrifice, but how beautiful to grow to be more like the One who sacrificed all for us!

The feminists would scream, "The issue is demanding your rights; then you are strong! It is not giving up your rights for another; then you are weak!" True strength is born when we sacrifice. A servant wife has a deep strength. The *natural* thing is to demand our rights, to assert *self*. The *supernatural* thing is to give our lives, to minister, to serve, to sacrifice. Christ, the servant leader, showed us the way. . . . My prayer for me, for you, is that we will follow in His steps.

I love you,
Mom

LEARNING TO GIVE IN TIME OF CRISIS

Dear Daughters,

Crises come wrapped in packages of all shapes and sizes. There are little boxes; in-between-size boxes; gigantic boxes; boxes labeled personal crisis, couple crisis, kid crisis, job crisis, everyday crisis, health crisis, life crisis. Webster defines *crisis* as "a situation that has reached a critical phase; an unstable or crucial time." In regard to the marriage relationship, I would like to define *crisis* as "those enemies from without that can rob you of oneness, the problems and stresses of life that descend on all of us."

My heart is heavy today as I write to you. We were told of a couple who were just told that their twenty-year-old daughter has two inoperable malignant tumors. How does a marriage survive a trial of this magnitude?

A dear friend is in personal crisis, seemingly unable to deal with issues in her past. Her husband told me the hardest part was to realize he couldn't "fix it." "I hurt so much for her," he said, "but at the same time I'm weary of the problem, angry that she won't deal with it and move on with life." How does a marriage survive a long drawn-out problem with no end in sight?

Crisis mode is no respecter of persons. Jesus said, "In the world you will have tribulation, but . . . I have overcome the world" (John 16:33). I've talked with more than one wife who

was shocked that Christian couples would experience crises, problems, and trials. This "if we trust Jesus, life and marriage will be one rosy glow" is nauseating.

When your grandmothers were newlyweds, their men went off to war, a long and bitter war. Living through the depression, agonizing through the war, they expected life to be difficult and were ready for it. Today, wars are fought and won in a few days, and many young women expect life to be won the same way. Trials, crises, may come to others but not to them, and if they should possibly be attacked, there surely is a quick, painless solution somewhere.

Even the marriage vows indicate that problems and times of crisis are a part of married life: "For better or worse, for richer or poorer, in sickness and in health."

The better, richer, and health parts sound good, but marriage also includes the other three: worse, poorer, and sickness. Do we really listen to *all* the vows when we repeat them? One married couple commented,

> Married life, after all, is not exclusively made up of picnics, dinners out, roses and surprise gifts. It's ordinary living with not enough money, too much work, too much stress in an uptight world. It's good stuff mixed with bad. If married partners believe their marriage is going to be just like their courtship, they'll find themselves continually frustrated.[6]

I hope you don't think this letter sounds morbid and depressing. The word I would use is *realistic*. Certainly, God does not want us sitting around waiting for illness, poverty, and the worse

of the marriage vows, but part of maturity is realizing that negative as well as positive circumstances are part of life and marriage, that there is no immunization shot against them. Crisis and trial, our enemies, cannot overwhelm and defeat us if we are prepared and know how to face them.

No place in Scripture are we promised a problem-free life. We are told that as Christians we have the Problem Solver living within. The One who created the heavens and earth knows us intimately and is deeply concerned that through the storms of life, we grow as individuals and as marriage partners. God never says the growth is pleasant; He says it is necessary.

I will write again soon to share with you some practical ways to deal with crisis and give you hope that even in the midst of crisis, you and your man can grow deeper in your oneness.

I love you,
Mom

WHAT DOES GOD WANT ME TO DO IN A CRISIS?

Dear Daughters,

We are in Hong Kong! What a strange and fascinating place! Although I am average height for an American, I feel foreign and big. Standing on the subway, I am taller than all the women and many of the men. Since I'm traveling to China tomorrow, I thought it appropriate to begin this letter with something from this difficult and interesting language. In Chinese, the word for

crisis is a combination of the symbols for *danger* plus *opportunity*. Applied to our marriages, in crisis there is either danger that we will let the crisis destroy our oneness or opportunity that our oneness will grow deeper and more beautiful through the trial.

As inevitable storms rumble through our lives, it is imperative that we turn to God and to each other, and that we assume personal responsibility for our choices during each crisis.

I'm sure you're tired of hearing your mom talk about choices. I have to keep saying it because our secret choices determine where we are headed. At no time is it so difficult to choose to love, to forgive, to encourage, to accept, than during a time of great stress and yet so necessary. The temptation is to withdraw from each other and try to handle our hurts, becoming self-centered. God wants you and me to do the difficult thing, to decide, "I will do my part to help our marriage team pull together during this crisis."

Recently, I talked to Barbara, a young woman who was facing the first big crisis in her marriage. She was down in the dumps and also dumping on her partner because *his* faults were so evident when crisis mode brought high tension to the relationship. Barbara's crisis was the house they were building. Everything had gone wrong, and both she and her husband, Stan, wished they had never decided on the building project. Because of the wrong estimate, they were under great financial stress, and it seemed every time they talked, the topic of conversation was the house, the house, and the house, which just increased the tension.

My first advice to Barbara was that she take personal responsibility for her part of the "dump routine," and make positive

choices. The house situation was not good, but her response was making it worse and causing the house crisis to become a marriage crisis.

Second, I shared with Barbara one practical suggestion of what we did during a time of great stress. Several years ago we had a trial, a kid crisis (of course, not anyone you know), and our relationship felt more like a teenage crisis center than a marriage. Every time we opened our mouths, it was, "What do you think we should do? How should we react? What should we say? Do you think this would help, and what about this?" We knew it was unhealthy for our relationship, but no matter what we began talking about, the conversation always came back around to the kid crisis. What is on your hearts will be on your lips. We felt like we didn't have a life, just a problem.

Our solution was to go away for a week alone and put a moratorium on the problem. Neither of us could talk about children; not one word could we utter! It was so refreshing! We were exhausted and too tired to ski on our ski vacation so couch potatoes we became. We watched a video series, vegetated, loved, relaxed, escaped, and it was wonderful!

By day six of our seven-day escape, we were able to look at each other and say, "Okay, now let's pray once again and seek wisdom from our God." We had gained a better perspective and could discuss the issues without the crisis possessing us.

I suggested to Barbara that she and her husband try to get away, at least for one night, to relax and love and forget about the house. The plans, financial stress, questions, and problems would still be there when they returned. Barbara said they felt

like they fell in love all over again. Their getaway was so invigorating that they decided to keep the house moratorium in place and only permitted themselves to talk "house talk" for a half hour a day!

Of course, some problems cannot be forgotten for a day, or for six days, but when possible, try this escape suggestion during your crisis. You will find it gets your eyes off the problem and on to God's working in the midst of the mess.

Love,
Mom

*G*OD'S PERSPECTIVE IN THE MIDST OF CRISIS

Dear Daughters,

In times of trial, God's perspective is what we need most, yet our hearts and minds seem geared to what we can see and touch. When what we are seeing goes from crisis to major crisis, we get stuck in our own perspective.

Chuck Swindoll talks about the "grind of human viewpoint." I love his writing because he always says it like it is:

Every waking moment of our lives we operate from one of two viewpoints: human or divine. I sometimes refer to these as horizontal perspective and vertical perspective. The more popular of the two is human. We much prefer to think, maintain our attitudes, and conduct our lives indepen-

dently. Human opinions influence us more than God's commands and principles. Horizontal solutions give us greater security and pleasure, unfortunately, than vertical ones. Rather than waiting on our Lord to solve our dilemma in His own time, we would normally choose the option of stepping in and manipulating a fast, painless escape.[7]

When we are faced with a trial, we much prefer taking a tangible way out instead of trusting God to see us through. It is easier to escape with our husbands and put a moratorium on the problem, even easier to try to take personal responsibility than to trust.

Trusting God during a crisis is difficult because we don't know how long the crisis will continue or what the outcome will be. We don't know how long we will have to trust. Trust is the answer to worry, but when a child has cancer, a business has gone bankrupt, or a beloved is in deep depression, the logical horizontal perspective is to worry. In Proverbs 3:5–6 (NASB), we are told how to trust in a practical way: what our part is in trusting and what God's part is. I have this passage glued to the crevices of my mind because it has been such an encouragement to me in time of crisis:

> Trust in the LORD with all your heart,
> And do not lean on your own understanding.
> In all your ways acknowledge Him,
> And He will make your paths straight.

In this passage there are four verbs, three directed at you, one toward God. Your part is to (1) "trust," (2) "not lean," and (3) "acknowledge," and God's part is to (4) "make your paths straight." One little word, the word *your,* is mentioned four times in these two verses. Your responsibility in a crisis situation is to

> trust with all *your* heart,
> refuse to lean on *your* understanding,
> acknowledge Him in all *your* ways,
> so that He might make straight *your* paths.

What do these four *yours* mean? First, "Trust with all your heart." For me, it means that I express my trust in God by thanking Him for the trial. First Thessalonians 5:18 declares, "In everything give thanks," so I say something like this: "Lord, this situation makes no sense to me. I don't understand it, but I thank You for it. By thanking You, I'm saying to You, I trust You to know better than I know. I trust You even though I can't see what You are doing. You promise that the results of trusting You in this situation are character, perseverance, and hope (Rom. 5:3–5)."

Second, "Do not lean on your own understanding." God says, "All things work together for good to those who love God, to those who are the called according to His purpose" (Rom. 8:28). You can respond, "Lord, I don't see how this crisis can work together for good, but I choose not to lean on what I can understand."

Third, "In all your ways acknowledge Him." *To acknowledge*

means "to recognize." Rather than leaning on your understanding, you acknowledge that God is the Blessed Controller of all things, even this trial.

Fourth, God "will make your paths straight." The Hebrew word means "to make smooth, straight, right." It includes the idea of removing obstacles that are in the way. God says His part is to straighten the stressful paths. He doesn't say when or how; He just promises He will.

A Green Beret came up to a speaker after listening to him discuss facing trials together as a couple and said, "In the Green Berets we train over and over, and then over and over again. We repeat some exercises until we are sick of them, but our instructors know what they are doing. They want us so prepared and finely trained that when trials and difficulties come on the battlefield, we will be able to fall back upon that which is second nature to us. We literally learn to do things by reflex action."[8]

We need to practice trusting, we need to practice not leaning, and we need to practice acknowledging in times of anxiety, in times of peace, in times of crisis, in times of joy. If we wait until the crisis mode hits, we'll worry instead of trust. The old horizontal perspective will take over because it's more natural to us as humans than the eternal perspective from God.

As wives, let's practice trusting until it becomes our instinctive response. Like the Green Berets, let's be prepared for crisis. Sometimes life seems to thrust us onto a battlefield, but God has given us the battle plan. This week, let's begin by memorizing Proverbs 3:5–6 and trust, do not lean, and acknowledge knowing that He will make straight our paths.

This letter may seem heavy, but read it again. It's one of the

most important you will receive from me. If as a couple, you and your husband will tackle your problems together with God's help, you will not fall apart but pull together.

Love,
Mom

P.S. I highly recommend the book *Trusting God Even When Life Hurts* by Jerry Bridges. It has been an encouragement to me in times of trial.

GROWING TOGETHER DURING CRISIS

Dear Daughters,

With four in college last year and three this year, the cupboards are beyond bare, and a camping trip was the most I could expect for an anniversary trip. What a wonderful surprise when our travel agent gave us two nights at the Budapest Hilton plus one three-course meal! Now I like camping, but an anniversary atop the walled part of old Budapest overlooking the blue Danube and picturesque Parliament building definitely won over the old rusty camper in the romance department.

Visions of Hungarian food eaten by candlelight, strolling musicians, and a view of incredible beauty . . . I was ready for all of it! We went camping on our honeymoon so the Hilton was definitely a step up, and I liked the step!

The view *was* breathtaking; the castle, Fisherman's Bastion, Mattias Church—all interesting. The food and music were all I'd anticipated; the moonlight walks overlooking the river were romantic. Everything was just right, all the physical circumstances

in place. There was romance, but the romance reflected the sadness of the romancers.

At one point your dad said, "I'm sorry this weekend has to be like this." When the get-a-way was planned, no one knew that Grampie would have just died, that our future would be totally uncertain, and that we would be experiencing one of the most difficult times of our life together. Not an atmosphere conducive to an anniversary celebration.

As we drove home, I told this man I'd loved for almost thirty years that I'd never felt closer to him. We had wept together, talked, and prayed; we had been silent together; and we had shared an intimacy that goes beyond words.

What does intimacy in marriage mean? Nancy Groom, in her book *Marriage Without Masks*, says that to experience true intimacy we must learn to identify and drop our masks, masks that we hide behind and that keep us from being vulnerable and honest and revealing our hidden selves.

I told your dad in Budapest about the mask book and suggested we read it together. He smiled and said, "But, Honey, we have no masks." No masks, no barriers, complete commitment and open lives create intimacy. And, too, I think that true intimacy is found in the hard times, when we cry, when answers evade us, when God seems far away, but we cling to Him and each other.

James said we are to welcome trials as friends for they produce character, perseverance, and hope. As individuals but also as marriage partners, we are to rejoice in the difficult things God allows in life and in the relationship. Applied to marriage, James 1 could be paraphrased, "Rejoice in the trials you face as a couple. They will teach you perseverance and make your love and commitment to each other strong. They will produce character, a strength that will lead to intimacy" (Mother Dillow's paraphrase).

I will always remember the anniversary trip, not because of the beautiful Danube but because of the intimacy amid the pain.

Love,
Mom

7

FORGIVENESS

*F*ACING UP TO OUR MISTAKES

Dear Daughters,

I blew it. Probably the most discouraging thing for me after all these years of marriage is to see myself make wrong choices when I know *exactly* what God wants me to do and exactly *how* to do it right. Yet in a moment of anger and frustration, I make the wrong choice, and royally blow it. I feel like a dog who has been disciplined for chewing the carpet and sneaks off with its tail between its legs.

No one disciplined me. I just knew I was wrong. Your father and I disagreed (that's a nice mild word), and he went off to sulk instead of resolving the problem. He was wrong, but so was I when I stormed into the room and told him he was selfish and didn't care about me or my feelings, only his own.

"Speak the truth in love," the Scripture says. Well, I spoke the truth all right, at least from my perspective, but in anger not in love. My wrong choice gave momentary relief (it genuinely feels good to tell someone off when you're angry), but what followed was the sickening realization that I had disobeyed God, I had made the situation worse, and I could have chosen a different path; to wait, pray, and at the right time, in the right place, and in the right way express my feelings and thoughts in *love*. I could have chosen to be wise instead of foolish.

Larry Crabb defines *wisdom* as the "belief that accepting God's

way, no matter how painful, leads ultimately to joy." He defines *foolishness* as "refusing to believe that going our own way, even though it genuinely relieves distress and feels good, leads ultimately to despair." How right he is. My eruption relieved distress and felt good for a moment but led to discouragement and disgust with myself. It could lead to despair, but I won't let it.

I was wrong. Oh, yes, the man in question was also wrong, but as I've said before, I'm responsible only for me, for my responses, for my choices. My husband is responsible before God for his. I made a wrong choice, so now I have another choice to make. I can sit and sulk: "Woe is me. I can't do anything right. I even wrote a book on marriage and just look at me. I might as well not try." Or I can confess, first to God, then to my husband: "I was wrong to explode in anger and say you were selfish. Will you forgive me?" Notice, I did not mention *his* sin, only my own. Confession is not an opportunity to again remind the one you love of his failings. It's tempting but wrong.

The devious type of confession goes something like this: "Because you were such a selfish creep, I exploded in anger. I was wrong. Will you forgive me?" Asking for forgiveness becomes yet another golden opportunity to point the finger and make sure our partners know the *only* reason we acted in anger is that they are so difficult to live with.

When we ask for forgiveness, we admit *our* wrong and only ours. We confess, then forget, and move on, asking God for strength and power with a new determination to make wise choices even when our emotions scream to do otherwise.

God's way *is* difficult, sometimes painful, but it *does* ultimately lead to joy. Often God is the only One who knows how deep the

struggle has been, how tough to not speak in anger but wait, pray, and speak in love. Often God is the only One who knows how hard it has been to forgive, but when we make the right choice in obedience, we find true joy!

I love you,
Mom

*F*IGHTING OVER NOTHING

Dear Daughters,

Rachel Jones takes the prize for the champion grudge holder of all time! Certainly, she should be in the *Guinness Book of World Records* under the auspicious title "Woman Who Holds Longest Grudge." It has been said that carrying a grudge is like being stung to death by one bee. If that's true, David Thomas was just one big bee sting!

Every week for forty-two years, David slipped a love letter under the door of his neighbor, Rachel Jones. Each letter attempted to mend the lovers' quarrel that parted them when both were thirty-two years old. The grudge-holding Rachel burned each letter, and she repeatedly refused to speak to her suitor.

Finally, despite the silent treatment, David summoned courage to knock on her door and propose, and to his surprise, she accepted. Both Rachel and David were *seventy-four years old* when they finally got married![1]

What did Rachel gain during her long years of silence? What did she achieve by failing to forgive? She gained loneliness, bitterness, and perhaps a sense of power over another person. Was

her vigilant stance of "I'm right and nothing will make me change my mind" worth forty-two years of anguish? I wish she were still alive so we could ask her.

I strongly suspect, however, that she would say she had wasted years for a "principle" that really mattered very little. How often we quarrel over things that are of such little significance! I know in our marriage I find it hard to remember the issues that made me furious just a month before. The following quote from the excellent book *For Lovers Only* puts our pettiness into perspective:

One of these days, much sooner than you want to face, one of you is going to be sitting beside the deathbed of the other, holding a frail, clammy hand. You'll look into each other's misty eyes during those aching, final hours, and the memories will flood through your grieving minds in a raging torrent.

You will not regret a single dreamy walk you took together in the park. You will not regret the time you stayed up so late talking and holding each other that you were both zombies at work the next day. You will not regret all the times you made love and let the housework go.

But I'll tell you what you will regret. You will regret the thousands of hours that you spent fighting over nothing. Oh, at the time it seemed like a big deal. At the time, you were both so worked up over those burning issues that you would have thought the fate of the free world hung in the balance. But on the last day you spend with your lover on this earth, you will see all the things you fought over for what they really were: nothing. Absolutely nothing.

On that day you won't care who got in the last word. On that day it won't matter one whit which of you finally got his way. On that day you won't even be able to remember what started 99 percent of the fights. All you'll remember is that it was priceless time irretrievably, foolishly lost.[2]

Love,
Mom

BREAKING THE CYCLE OF BLAME AND PAIN

Dear Daughters,

I was thinking today about that song, popular a few years ago, "Love Is Never Having to Say You're Sorry." What a totally inaccurate, meaningless, and just plain stupid title! Love, in reality, is learning to say I'm sorry often, learning to swallow pride and selfishness, and learning to forgive.

A happy marriage is the union of two good forgivers who have committed to not hold a grudge and nurse a hurt. Instead each freely forgives the other, even though sometimes the other does not "deserve" forgiveness.

That is easy to write but very difficult to accomplish, especially when you are the wounded or misunderstood party.

In the book *Love in the Time of Cholera* by Nobel laureate Gabriel Garcia Marquez, a marriage is portrayed that disintegrates over a bar of soap. It was the wife's job to keep the house in order, including the towels, toilet paper, and soap in the bathroom. One

day she forgot to replace the soap, an oversight her husband mentioned in an exaggerated way ("I've been bathing for almost a week without any soap") but she vigorously denied. Although she had indeed forgotten, her pride was at stake, and she would not back down. What was the outcome of one bar of soap not being in the bathroom? For the next seven months, they slept in separate rooms and ate in silence.

Marquez writes, "They were very careful about bringing it up, even after years had passed and they were old, for the barely healed wounds could begin to bleed again as if they had been inflicted only yesterday."[3]

How can a bar of soap ruin a marriage? Because neither partner would say, "Stop. This cannot go on. I'm sorry. Forgive me." Over such trivialities, lifelong relationships crack apart, and only forgiveness can halt the widening fissures.

For us, forgiveness is unnatural, but for God, forgiveness is natural. He is by nature free from the pride and selfishness that by nature are our nature. God forgave us in Christ "while we were still sinners," when we were undeserving, when we turned our backs on Him (Rom. 5:8). Not only does He forgive, but He forgets our sin. He promises, "Their sin I will remember no more" (Jer. 31:34).

God asks us to forgive as He has forgiven us, not once or twice but seventy times seven. He must have had marriage in mind when He said that because in this most intimate encounter we are most vulnerable and open to hurt and we need the most often to forgive.

If a friend wounds or hurts you, it is painful, but if your

partner—chosen for life, the one who knows all your warts and failings—wounds you, the hurt is deeper. And so often, it is most difficult to be a forgiver with the one you love the most.

The couple in Garcia Marquez's novel had become prisoners because of their unwillingness to forgive, and all over a bar of soap! Surely, we would not be so petty and immature . . . I hope not, but I'm not sure. I have counseled many women whose marriages were in shambles, who had allowed an insignificant incident between husband and wife to blow up into a full-scale civil war.

I began this letter by saying that a good marriage is the union of two good forgivers. It has been helpful for me to write this letter and be forced to think about my responses. I laughed to myself about the bar of soap episode, but with my laughter came an inward cringing that I also had made issues over trivia. How clear it becomes when one really thinks about it. It is my choice: Do I forgive, or do I choose to hold a grudge?

I love you,
Mom

$\mathcal{K}$EEPING NO RECORD OF WRONGS

Dear Joy and Robin,

I was thinking today about Ephesians 4:32: "And be kind to one another, tender-hearted, forgiving one another, just as God in Christ also forgave you." How wonderful our marriages would be if we could apply just this one verse!

As husbands and wives, we need the healing touch of forgive-

ness. Where else could there be more opportunity to annoy, insult, or offend than in the most intimate of relationships, marriage?

Dr. Ed Wheat affirms that newlyweds need to develop the "skill" of forgiving each other. Forgiveness is not a feeling but a choice we make, and often it goes against every self-centered fiber of our being. This choice is vividly seen in this story told about Clara Barton, the founder of the American Red Cross. One day she was reminded of a vicious deed that someone had done to her years before. But she acted as if she had never heard of the incident! "Don't you remember it?" her friend asked. "No" came Barton's reply. "I distinctly remember forgetting it."[4] A conscious choice to forgive a vicious deed, a conscious choice to continue forgiving when reminded of the deed. By replying, "I distinctly remember forgetting it," Clara Barton was saying, "I remember choosing to forgive, and I still choose to forgive."

Did her choice eliminate all pain caused by the horrible act? Certainly not; but her words portray a woman at peace, a woman who was able to love because she forgave. First Corinthians 13:5 maintains that "love keeps no record of wrongs" (NIV). To love and forgive, we must

1. Choose with our free will to forgive.
2. Make the promise to lift the burden of guilt from the person as far as the wrong against you is concerned. Remember the person's sin no more, never naming it again to the person, to others, or to yourself.
3. Seal it with your behavior, demonstrating love with tenderhearted kindness.

4. Trust God to allow you to forget and to renew your mind with new attitudes.[5]

The following story has been an encouragement to me to follow these four steps:

When missionaries first went to the Eskimos, they could not find a word in their language for forgiveness so they had to compound one. This turned out to be ISSUMAGJOU-JUNGNAINERMIK! It is a formidable looking group of letters but an expression that has a beautiful connotation for those who understand it. It means "Not-being-able-to-think-about-it-anymore." I have this huge word "ISSU-MAGJOUJUNGNAINERMIK" posted in large letters on my refrigerator. I get some strange looks when people see it but it reminds me to forgive freely and forget, to not be able to think about it anymore.[6]

My prayer for you, my daughters, and for me is that we might be faithful to choose to be good forgivers; that our marriages might be characterized by forgiveness, kindness, and tenderness.

Much love,
Mom

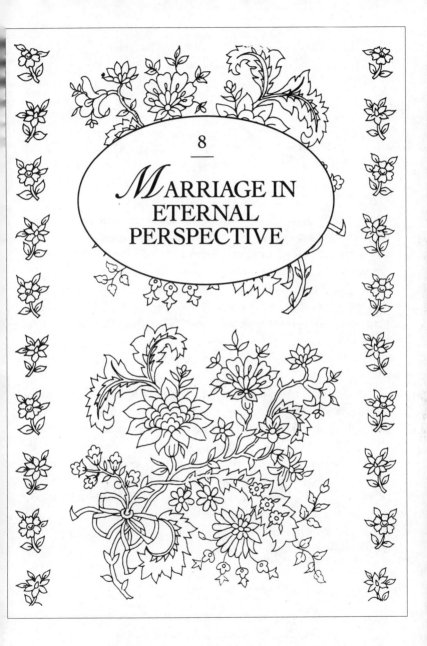

8

*M*ARRIAGE IN
ETERNAL
PERSPECTIVE

ℋOW DO WE LIVE EACH DAY AS A GIFT OF GOD?

Dear Daughters,

You've thought about many aspects of marriage, I am sure, but looking at marriage from an eternal perspective is probably not one of them. It somehow doesn't sound as romantic and exciting as love, honeymoon, sex . . . the good stuff!

First, what is *perspective?* The term, according to Webster, literally suggests "looking through . . . seeing clearly, the capacity to view things in their true relation of relative importance." I like to think of perspective as a way of seeing. An eternal perspective, then, is God's way of seeing, viewing your marriage and what is important from God's perspective.

For the next few minutes, snap a telescopic lens on your perspective and pull yourself up close, close enough to see the real you, the bride in shimmering white. Now, view your life as a wife clearly. You are at the beginning of marriage, looking forward. What an exciting place to be! But someday you will be at the end of your marriage, looking back. The hope is that the end will be as exciting as the beginning, even *more* exciting! To gain perspective, you need to see marriage in its totality. Three things are necessary to gain God's perspective on your role as a wife, to see clearly down through the years:

1. Live each day as a gift of God.
2. Live with the end in view.
3. Live to be faithful to Christ.

To live each day in light of time is to realize that love is a gift from God, that this man beside me is a gift. To realize that God has given me only a certain number of days on this earth to love my husband, to share together, to grow in our intimate oneness, to be lovers and best friends. Because our days are short, it is good to repeat and remember these words of Scripture: "Teach us to number our days and recognize how few they are; help us to spend them as we should" (Ps. 90:12 TLB).

Each wife has a limited amount of time in the classroom of love with her husband. It may be five years or fifty years. I've been privileged, thus far, to have almost twenty-nine years with my lover and best friend. No matter how many years we have to grow in our intimate oneness, the time is short. When we realize this, *really* realize it, it can change the way we look at time, at love, and at our lovers. Sadly, many wives discover too late the gift they possessed. One such wife is seen in the Pulitzer prize–winning drama *Our Town*.

Emily, the young wife in the drama, died at age twenty-six but was allowed the privilege of returning to an ordinary day from her past life. However, with the opportunity, she was warned: "At least choose an unimportant day. Choose the least important day in your life. It will be important enough."

She chose to relive her twelfth birthday, but soon she cried, "I can't. I can't go on. It goes so fast. We don't have time to look at

one another. I didn't realize. So all that was going on and we never noticed."

Another character commented from the grave, "Yes, that's what it was to be alive. To move about in a cloud of ignorance; to go up and down trampling on the feelings of those about you. To spend and waste time as though you had a million years. To be always at the mercy of one self-centered passion or another."

But Emily's question pierces the heart: "Do any human beings ever realize life while they live it?"[1] The answer is no.

We're encouraged in the Scriptures to not waste time as if we had a million years, but to realize life is short:

> Live life, then, with a due sense of responsibility, not as men who do not know the meaning and purpose of life but as those who do. Make the best use of your time, despite all the difficulties of these days. Don't be vague but firmly grasp what you know to be the will of the Lord. (Eph. 5:15–17 PHILLIPS)

I've often thought that if we knew exactly how many hours, days, and years we had together, we might be more aware of the importance of each choice we make, but God has not chosen to let us know. Dr. Ed Wheat's advice to us is, "So live and so love your partner as though it were your last day to enjoy the gift of time together."[2]

I love you,
Mom

$\mathcal{H}$OW DO WE LIVE WITH THE END IN VIEW?

Dear Daughters,

I want to take you on a journey with me, a journey through your life as a wife. The best way to do this is to take you to a funeral. Now don't put the letter down. I assure you that I have not lost my mind and I know what I'm doing.

Imagine you are going to the funeral of a loved one. Picture yourself driving to the church, parking the car, and getting out. As you enter the church, you hear your favorite hymn being played; you see the faces of friends and family and feel the sorrow of losing, the joy of having known that is so evident on their faces.

As you walk to the front of the church and look inside the casket, you suddenly come face-to-face with yourself. With disbelief, you realize that it is your funeral, fifty years from today. The people gathered together are here to express their love and appreciation for your life. Numb with shock, you are led to a seat and handed a program.

You look at the program in your hand and see that there is to be a speaker—your husband. Now think long and hard. What would you like your husband to say about you after fifty years of marriage? What character qualities would you like him to have

seen in you? What kind of love would you want him to have received from you during all those years?

As you think deeply about these questions, write down your thoughts and feelings, and keep the piece of paper because what you have written is *your* definition of the wife you desire to become.

To live your life with the end in view is to begin today with the image of the end of your life as your frame of reference. Each part of your life—what you do today, tomorrow, next week, next year; how you choose to spend the time with your lover—can be examined in the context of the whole, of what really matters most to you.

It is very difficult to think about the end of anything when you are at the beginning. I'm past the midpoint, headed toward the home stretch, and it's still difficult. We are "daily" people, not lifetime people, but God wants us to be eternal people. How I wish someone had asked me to visualize my funeral at the beginning; it helps put all we hope and desire into perspective.

Ultimately, my greatest desire is to be found faithful to my God. What does God require of me as a wife? First Corinthians 4:2 asserts, "It is required of [a wife] that she be found faithful," not successful, not popular, but faithful. I live my years as a wife knowing that one day the Lord will ask me, "Were you faithful to do your part, to love your man, to make the right choices?" I long to hear the Lord say, "Well done, good and faithful servant."

Keep looking up. That's where God's perspective is! He has

set eternity in our hearts so that we might look beyond the routine of life and realize life while we live it.

Much love,
Mom

*T*HE PURSUIT OF EXCELLENCE

Dear Daughters,

In the first letter I wrote you about loving your man, it was your father's and my anniversary. Amazingly enough, it's anniversary time again. God gives us anniversaries as milestones, significant points in the passing of time, specific yet mute reminders that more sand has passed through the hourglass. God builds them into our calendars once every year to enable us to make an annual appraisal not of the *length* of time we've been married but the *depth* of our intimacy, not just to remind us we've been married *longer* but to help us determine if we are now married *deeper*.

Anniversaries do, however, give us a handle on the measurement of time. Another year has passed for me. It truly seems unbelievable that I've been writing these letters to you for a year! The minutes of marriage pass so quietly, so consistently, that we fail to realize the time is ticking away. We have only this year, this month, this moment to love. Picture your life of seventy years as a clock with the hours of a single day from seven in the morning until midnight.

You, my daughters, are almost at noon, in the sunlight time of life. I'm just past 6:00 P.M., headed toward evening. Yet, how

clearly I remember my wedding day. Was it really twenty-nine years ago? How quickly the hands of the clock move around the circle. We must not move about in a cloud of ignorance, spending and wasting time as though we had a million years. We must be women who realize life while we live it!

> Four things come not back,
> The spoken word, the sped arrow,
> Time past, the neglected opportunity.

We can't bring time back, but we can seize the opportunity today to live each day as a gift of God: seeking to love, seeking to encourage, seeking to give, seeking excellence.

We Must Live with the End in View

To begin with the end in view means to start your marriage with a clear understanding of your destination as a wife. By keeping that end clearly in view, you can make certain that whatever you do on any particular day does not go against the criteria you have defined as supremely important, and that each day of your life contributes in a meaningful way to your vision of your life as a whole.[3]

To help you think about the end at the beginning, I took you on a journey to your own funeral fifty years from now and asked you these questions: What would you like your husband to say about you after fifty years of marriage? What kind of wife would you want his words to present? What character qualities would you like him to have seen in you? What kind of love relationship

would you want him to describe? What kind of love would you want him to have received from you during all those years?

In Proverbs 31, we have a beautiful example of a woman of excellence, the virtuous woman. Her husband praised her after thirty or more years of marriage. And what a tribute his praise was:

> Many women have done excellently,
> But you excel them all. (Prov. 31:29 paraphrased)

It's as if her husband said, "For thirty years I've watched women, seen the wives of my friends, I've intimately known you, my wife. I've seen your strengths, your weaknesses: but after observing all women, it is very obvious to me, *you* excel them all."

Aristotle said, "We are what we repeatedly do." Excellence, then, is not an act but a habit. Our character, who we are *becoming*, is basically a composite of our habits.

> Sow a thought, reap an action;
> Sow an action, reap a habit;
> Sow a habit, reap an attitude;
> Sow an attitude; reap a character;
> Sow a character, reap a destiny.

A personal marriage statement can set us on the right path to becoming women of excellence. Adhering to it determines where we are headed, who we will become. Our secret choices determine our thoughts, which determine our words, actions, habits,

attitude, character, and destiny; who we become. The Proverbs 31 wife became the most excellent of all, and the reason is clear; it is visible for all to see:

> Charm is deceitful and beauty is vain,
> But a woman who fears the LORD,
>   she shall be praised.
> Give her of the fruit of her hands,
> And let her own works praise her in
>   the gates. (Prov. 31:30–31)

The excellent wife had as part of her personal marriage statement to view her marriage with an eternal perspective; she lived in fear and reverence of God, and she lived to be faithful to her God. Her eternal focus plus her secret choices determined her destiny.

We Must Live to Be Faithful to Christ

Paul wrote, "I press toward the goal for the prize of the upward call of God in Christ Jesus" (Phil. 3:14).

Chuck Swindoll puts this verse in perspective:

Our ultimate goal, our highest calling in life, is to glorify God, not to be happy. Let that sink in! Glorifying Him is our greatest pursuit. Not to get our way. Not to be comfortable. Not to find fulfillment. Not even to be loved or to be appreciated or to be taken care of. Now these are important, but they are not primary.

As I glorify Him, He sees to it that other essential needs are met . . . or my need for them diminishes. Believe me, this concept will change your entire perspective on yourself, your life, and your marriage.[4]

As I look at the hands of the clock of life and see that my life is more than half over, that I am headed down the home stretch, I realize that I desire two things above all else:

1. To hear my Lord say to me, "Well done, good and faithful servant."
2. To know that during all the years of my marriage I have strived to live my personal marriage statement.

W. Nathaniel Howell was ambassador to Kuwait and withstood four and one-half months of virtual imprisonment at the American embassy during the Gulf War. People frequently ask him, "Were you afraid?" Howell's answer:

We would have been fools if we hadn't been afraid at times. But what it taught me about myself was that I was a whole lot more afraid of not being able to live with myself if I didn't do what was right, than I was of Saddam Hussein and his troops. You only die once, but you live with yourself a long time.[5]

My daughters, for you, for me, I desire that we will not only be able to live with ourselves, but that we will live with peace and

joy knowing that we have made the secret choices that are honoring to God, and that build an intimate oneness with our husbands.

This week, your father and I were at a dinner party, and a man said to me, "Linda, I hear you are writing another book on marriage. There are so many books on marriage in Christian bookstores, how is this one unique?" Before I could answer, your father answered for me and said, "My wife's book is powerful because she has lived what she is saying." I was very humbled by his comment because I know how far I still have to go to become the wife I desire to be.

My prayer for you, my daughters, is that you, too, might be praised by your husbands after many years of marriage and hear the beautiful words:

> Many women have done excellently,
> But you excel them all!

I love you,
Mom

NOTES

Chapter 1

1. Stephen R. Covey, *The 7 Habits of Highly Effective People* (New York: Simon and Schuster, 1989), 99.

2. Paul Lee Tan, *Encyclopedia of 7700 Illustrations* (Rockville, Md.: Assurance Publishers, 1979), 326.

3. Elisabeth Elliot, *Let Me Be a Woman* (Wheaton, Ill.: Tyndale, 1976), 10.

4. Michael P. Green, *Illustrations for Biblical Preaching* (Grand Rapids, Mich.: Baker, 1982), 220.

5. Lawrence J. Crabb, Jr., and Dan B. Allender, *Encouragement: The Key to Caring* (Grand Rapids, Mich.: Zondervan, 1984), 52.

6. Ed Wheat, M.D., *Secret Choices* (Grand Rapids, Mich.: Zondervan, 1989), 11.

7. Ibid., 15–16.

8. Ibid., 16.

Chapter 2

1. Willard F. Harley, Jr., *His Needs, Her Needs* (Old Tappan, N.J.: Revell, 1986).

2. *Why Women Want More Love, Why Men Want More Sex* .

3. Paul Lee Tan, *Encyclopedia of 7700 Illustrations* (Rockville, Md.: Assurance Publishers, 1979), 463.

4. R. Paul Stevens, *Getting Ready for a Great Marriage* (Colorado Springs: NavPress, 1990), 20.

5. Mike Mason, *The Mystery of Marriage* (Portland, Oreg.: Multnomah, 1985), 47.

6. William J. Peterson, *C. S. Lewis Had a Wife* (Wheaton, Ill.: Tyndale, 1987), 174–75.

7. Stevens, *Getting Ready*, 36–37.

8. Stevens, *Getting Ready*, 19.

9. Dr. James Dobson, *Focus on the Family Magazine*, February, 1986.

Chapter 3

1. Lawrence J. Crabb, Jr., and Dan B. Allender, *Encouragement: The Key to Caring* (Grand Rapids, Mich.: Zondervan, 1984), 10.

2. Ibid., 20.

3. Bill Hull, *Right Thinking* (Colorado Springs: NavPress, 1985), 76.

4. Michael P. Green, *Illustrations for Biblical Preaching* (Grand Rapids, Mich.: Baker, 1989), 119.

5. Paul Lee Tan, *Encyclopedia of 7700 Illustrations* (Rockville, Md.: Assurance Publishers, 1979), 1422.

6. Ibid., 1424.

7. Ibid., 71.

Chapter 4

1. *The Greenville News*, 26 April 1981, 19A.

2. Norman Wright, *Communication: Key to Your Marriage* (Glendale, CA.: Regal Books, 1974)

3. Nancy Groom, *Married Without Masks* (Colorado Springs: NavPress, 1989), 137–38.

4. Alan Loy McGinnis, *The Friendship Factor* (Minneapolis: Augsburg, 1979), 103–4.

Chapter 5

1. *Ladies' Home Journal*.

2. "Dear Abby," *The Stars and Stripes*, 16 and 17 September 1991.

3. Stephen and Judith Schwambach, *For Lovers Only* (Eugene, Oreg.: Harvest House, 1990), 127.

4. Linda Dillow, *Creative Counterpart* (Nashville: Thomas Nelson, 1986), 196.

5. Arndt and Gingrich, *A Greek-English Lexicon of the New Testament* (Grand Rapids, Mich.: Zondervan, 1957), 440.

6. *The International Standard Bible Encyclopedia* (Grand Rapids, Mich.: Eerdmans, 1988), s.v. "sodomite." See Lev. 18:22; 20:13.

7. *Theological Wordbook of the Old Testament* (Chicago: Moody Press, 1980), 2:788.

8. Ibid., s.v. "crime."

9. *The Lexicon Webster Dictionary*, 2 vols (English Language Institute of America, 1976), 2:922.

10. Schwambach, *For Lovers Only*, 154.

11. Linda Dillow, *Creative Counterpart* (Nashville: Thomas Nelson, 1977), 202.

12. Joseph C. Dillow, *Solomon on Sex* (Nashville: Thomas Nelson, 1977), 145.

13. Dr. Frank and Mary Alice Minirth, Dr. Brian and Dr. Deborah Newman, Dr. Robert and Susan Hemfelt, *Passages of Marriage* (Nashville: Thomas Nelson, 1991), 45.

14. Willard F. Harley, Jr., *His Needs, Her Needs* (Old Tappan, N.J.: Revell, 1986), 10.

Chapter 6

1. Dennis Rainey, *Lonely Husbands, Lonely Wives* (Dallas: Word, 1989), 73.

2. Ibid., 51.

3. Ibid.

4. Paul Lee Tan, *Encyclopedia of 7700 Illustrations* (Rockville, Md.: Assurance Publishers, 1979), 573.

5. Christopher Lasch, *The Culture of Narcissism* (New York: Norton, 1979), 72, 22.

6. Jim and Sally Conway, *Traits of a Lasting Marriage* (Downers Grove, Ill.: InterVarsity, 1991), 27.

7. Charles R. Swindoll, *Living Beyond the Daily Grind* (Dallas: Word, 1988), 156.

Chapter 7

1. Paul Lee Tan, *Encyclopedia of 7700 Illustrations* (Rockville, Md.: Assurance Publishers, 1979), 284.

2. Stephen and Judith Schwambach, *For Lovers Only* (Eugene, Oreg.: Harvest House, 1990), 19–20.

3. Philip Yancey, "The Unnatural Act," *Christianity Today*, 8 April 1991, 37.

4. Clara Barton, used by Luis Palau in the message "Experiencing God's Forgiveness."

5. Wheat, *First Years of Forever*, 47–48.

6. Tan, *7700 Illustrations*, 456.

Chapter 8

1. Thornton Wilder, *Our Town: A Play in Three Acts* (New York: Harper and Row, 1957), from Act 3.

2. Ed Wheat, M.D., *The First Years of Forever* (Grand Rapids, Mich.: Zondervan, 1988), 177.

3. Stephen R. Covey, *The 7 Habits of Highly Effective People* (New York: Simon and Schuster, 1989), 98.

4. Charles R. Swindoll, *Strike the Original Match* (Portland, Oreg.: Multnomah, 1980), 165.

5. *USA Today*, 16 December 1991, 2.